Steam Power

by Brian Solomon

Voyageur Press

To Richard Gruber, a lifelong steam enthusiast.

First published in 2009 by MBI Publishing Company and Voyageur Press, an imprint of MBI Publishing Company, 400 First Avenue North, Suite 300, Minneapolis, MN 55401 USA

Voyageur Press titles are also available at discounts in bulk quantity for industrial or sales-promotional use. For details write to Special Sales Manager at MBI Publishing Company, 400 First Avenue North, Suite 300, Minneapolis, MN 55401 USA.

To find out more about our books, visit us online at www.voyageurpress.com.

Library of Congress Cataloging-in-Publication Data

Solomon, Brian, 1966–
  Steam power / Brian Solomon. – 1st ed.
    p. cm.
  Includes bibliographical references and index.
  ISBN 978-0-7603-3336-5 (sb : alk. paper)
  1. Steam locomotives. 2. Steam locomotives–History.
I. Title.
  TJ603.S67 2009
  625.26'1–dc22
                                2008046172

Frontispiece: Sweden's B-class 4-6-0 is related to the Prussian Railways P-8 4-6-0 design of 1906. Of the 100-plus examples built—98 for SJ (Swedish Railways)—an estimated 48 are extant. One of these was exported to the United States in the 1990s. Equipped with a pair of pilot-mounted snowplows, the Belfast & Moosehead Lake No. 1149 worked for a dozen years in excursion service and was named the *Spirit of Unity* after the Maine town where it was based. Steam excursions were suspended in 2008 following a period of declining ridership. *Brian Solomon*

Title pages: The Canadian National Railway system, including U.S. subsidiary the Grand Trunk Western, operated the largest roster of 4-8-4s—203 locomotives. Typical of the CNR's late-era 4-8-4s is No. 6218, a Class U-2-g built by Alco's Canadian affiliate, Montreal Locomotive Works, in September 1942. On a flawless autumn day in 1964, it leads an excursion in Quebec. *Richard Jay Solomon*

Editor: Dennis Pernu
Designer: Wendy R. Lutge

Printed in China

Acknowledgments: This book could not have been possible without the assistance of many people. Special thanks to the participating photographers: John Gruber, Chris Guss, Tom Kline, George Kowanski, and Richard Jay Solomon. In addition, I am grateful to the following: Ed Beaudette, Kurt Bell, Joe Bispo, Steve Bogan, Scott Bontz, Robert A. Buck, George C. Corry, Stella Costello, Isabelle Dijols, David Dunn, Doug Eisele, Ken Fox, Mike Gardner, Richard Gruber, Paul Hammond, John P. Hankey, John Hartman, David Hegarty, Nona Hill, Stephen Hirsch, Tom A. Hoover, Tom S. Hoover, Bob Hoppe, Brian L. Jennison, Clark Johnson, George Legler, Denis McCabe, Patrick McKnight, Mel Patrick, Dennis Pernu, Dan Renehan, Tony Renehan, Peter Rigney, Staci M. Roy, Maureen Solomon, Séan Solomon, Hassard Stacpoole, Keith Thomasson, M. Ross Valentine, Harry Vallas, Otto Vondrak, Kevin Walker, and Ed Williams.

Contents

Introduction   6

Chapter 1   Building Eastern Industry   12

Chapter 2   Trains Across the Plains   74

Chapter 3   Taming the West   112

Chapter 4   Steam in Europe   158

Bibliography   188

Index   190

Introduction

Introduction

The locomotive was one of the foremost products of the Industrial Revolution. The steam locomotive had evolved in Britain from stationary industrial engines. Richard Trevithick demonstrated his pioneer locomotive at the Pen-y-Darran Iron Works in Wales on February 13, 1804. Over the next two decades, various small locomotives were built for operation on short industrial tramways. George Stephenson's Stockton & Darlington Railway opened in 1821. Considered the first public railway, it used locomotives to haul freight and passengers, establishing a pattern of operation rapidly copied across Britain and exported to the United States.

Equally influential was Stephenson's Liverpool & Manchester Railway (L&M), opened in 1829. To forward locomotive design, the L&M held a locomotive competition. The winning machine was the *Rocket*, built by Stephenson's son Robert. Its overwhelming success was due to its use of three basic locomotive design principles: a multi-tubular (fire tube) boiler, forced draft from exhaust steam, and direct linkage between the piston and drive wheels. This prototype established the foundation for most subsequent successful steam locomotive designs, not just in Britain, but around the world.

America was only a few years behind Britain in adopting the steam railway. In the 1820s, American engineers traveled across the Atlantic to study and import the new technology. In 1827, the Delaware & Hudson Canal Company planned a coal tramway from the mines near Carbondale, Pennsylvania, to its canal head at Honesdale. The D&H's Horatio Allen traveled to Britain and imported both rails and four complete locomotives for use on this primordial American line. At least one of the locomotives was fired up, but it proved an inauspicious beginning for steam in America, as these locomotives were deemed too heavy for regular operation and never performed as intended.

Within a few years, other railroads were underway. Some followed D&H's lead and imported British locomotives; others bought locomotives built locally. While some American locomotives used homegrown designs, the vast majority were technological descendants of Stephenson's Rocket. By the mid-1830s, several locomotive manufacturers had been established in the United States. The most significant, and ultimately the largest, was Philadelphia's Baldwin Locomotive Works.

American locomotives needed to fulfill different requirements than their British counterparts and followed a different evolutionary path. Often using tracks constructed to lower standards than in Britain, American locomotives required leading guide wheels and substantial pilots to keep from derailing. Also, American railroads looked to achieve ever greater levels of operating efficiency, and most didn't suffer from the variety of operating constraints that limited boiler size in Britain. In the twentieth century, locomotive size and output were pushed to the limit. Ultimately, American railroads operated some of the largest, heaviest, and most powerful steam locomotives ever built.

The desire for greater efficiency led American railroads to abandon steam, first on a small scale in favor of electric motive power, and then on a wide scale in favor of diesel-electric locomotives. Following World War II, diesels were ready for mass production and railroads began the expensive conversion to diesel operations. The last commercial steam locomotives were delivered in the late 1940s, and a small number of railroads resisted the conversion to diesel for a few years. Most notably, the Norfolk & Western (N&W) continued to build its own steam locomotives until the early 1950s. Nationally, by the mid-1950s, the once ubiquitous steam locomotive was becoming increasingly rare. Even the N&W recognized the superior economics of the diesel-electric, and in 1960 concluded its revenue main-line steam operations. The steam era was over, although isolated pockets of steam survived on a handful of short lines for a few more years.

The switch to diesel power occurred at the same time the railroads were losing their transport supremacy. Although freight remained important in many areas, the rapid decline of intercity passenger services after World War II changed public perception of the railroad. By the 1960s, there emerged nostalgia for steam locomotives. Some railroads had set aside steam locomotives for preservation. Other locomotives were acquired by individuals, museums, and communities for display and a few for operation. Of the estimated 138,000 steam locomotives built for U.S. railways, approximately 1,900 escaped scrapping. The majority of these are relatively small switchers and light freight locomotives built in the first decades of the twentieth century. Sadly, relatively few of the earliest machines survived and only select examples of the largest, fastest, and most impressive locomotives of the late steam era were preserved.

Over the years, a small number of preserved locomotives have been restored to operating condition for excursion services. Typically, these units are operated seasonally by railway museums or tourist railways. A few large locomotives have been restored for main-line trips. Although steam locomotives are comparatively simple machines, it is an extremely expensive proposition to maintain one in operating condition. Locomotives require periodic overhauls of the boiler, firebox, and other key components. Most surviving steam

Previous pages:
Consolidation No. 40 left Pennsylvania's Baldwin Locomotive Works in November 1925 for South Carolina's Lancaster & Chester Railroad. Today, it's much closer to its birthplace on the New Hope & Ivyland, a meandering 17-mile-long short line connecting its namesake towns in southeastern Pennsylvania. On a damp June afternoon, No. 40 storms up the grade out of New Hope. *Brian Solomon*

locomotives are at least 70 years old (many are much older) and occasionally develop problems that are costly to correct.

Today, the roster of working steam is like a big game of musical chairs. A locomotive that has worked for decades may be withdrawn from service and placed on static display. Other locomotives, cold since diesels made them redundant, may be returned to service. Some steam locomotives have regularly worked for years; others have made only occasional appearances. Of the many machines featured in this book, most have seen service since the end of revenue steam, although some are no longer in service as of this writing. These locomotives may operate again, provided there are sufficient interest, finances, and know-how to put them back into action.

The last chapter of this book focuses on steam power overseas, especially in Britain. Not only did the locomotive originate in Britain, but Britain has the most intensive and comprehensive railway preservation culture in the world. There, dozens of historic railways operate beautifully restored steam locomotives to the thrill of the public.

Steam was through on most American railways by the early to mid-1950s. By the early 1960s, a groundswell of railway enthusiasm brought steam back for excursion services. Where a steam locomotive wouldn't have earned a passing glance from the public a generation earlier, it was now a nostalgic attraction. In July 1966, enthusiasts scramble for the best angle of Burlington No. 4960 at Walnut, Illinois. *John Gruber*

Whyte Classification System

The most common American method of classifying steam locomotives is the Whyte system. Locomotive types are described by the arrangement of leading, driving, and trailing wheels. A zero indicates absence of wheels in one of these locations. For example, the classic American type, which has four leading wheels, four driving wheels, and no trailing wheels, is designated a 4-4-0. The Atlantic type has four leading wheels, four driving wheels, and two trailing wheels and is designated 4-4-2. Locomotives such as Mallets and Duplexes, which have more than one set of drivers and running gear, count each grouping of driving wheels. The Union Pacific Big Boy is so classified as a 4-8-8-4. Locomotives with built-in tanks rather than tenders have a letter "T" following the wheel count (for example, 0-6-0T).

The standard wheel arrangements have names associated with them. Early names were descriptive, such as the 4-6-0 Ten-Wheeler, but later names tended to represent the railroad that first used the arrangement. The 4-8-4, generally known as a Northern type after the Northern Pacific, is also known by a host of other names.

Wheel Arrangement	Whyte Classification	Name
<OOO	0-6-0	—
<ooOO	4-4-0	American
<ooOOo	4-4-2	Atlantic
<oOOO	2-6-0	Mogul
<oOOOo	2-6-2	Prairie
<ooOOO	4-6-0	Ten-Wheeler
<ooOOOo	4-6-2	Pacific
<ooOOOoo	4-6-4	Hudson
<oOOOO	2-8-0	Consolidation
<oOOOOo	2-8-2	Mikado
<oOOOOoo	2-8-4	Berkshire
<ooOOOO	4-8-0	Twelve-Wheeler
<ooOOOOo	4-8-2	Mountain
<ooOOOOoo	4-8-4	Northern
<oOOOOO	2-10-0	Decapod
<oOOOOOo	2-10-2	Santa Fe
<oOOOOOoo	2-10-4	Texas
<ooOOOOOOo	4-12-2	Union Pacific
<ooOOO OOOoo	4-6-6-4	Challenger
<ooOOOO OOOOoo	4-8-8-4	Big Boy

Chapter 1
Building Eastern Industry

Building Eastern Industry

The first North American railways were built in the East. These railways served established cities and towns, and were instrumental in the emergence of the eastern industrial manufacturing economy. Railroad companies competed for territory, often building parallel and overlapping infrastructure to reach the most lucrative sources of traffic, resulting in by far the most intensive railway network on the continent. Lines tapped coal and iron mines, timber stands, limestone quarries, and dozens of other resources. Intensive commuter services were developed around Boston, New York, and Philadelphia. Long-distance passenger trains connected virtually every community in the East. The busiest railroads required four-track main lines to accommodate the high volume of freight and passenger traffic. Secondary routes and branch lines were built to virtually every town of significant size, while trunk lines reached from eastern cities to gateways in the Midwest.

As the railroad network expanded and companies vied for traffic and territory, locomotive design progressed. Ever larger, faster, more powerful, and, ultimately, more efficient machines were built. In the nineteenth century, dozens of manufacturers built locomotives commercially. The largest manufacturers were Baldwin Locomotive Works in Philadelphia, Pennsylvania, established in 1831; the Schenectady Locomotive Works in Schenectady, New York, established in 1848; and Brooks Locomotive Works in Dunkirk, New York, established in 1869. Baldwin emerged as the largest builder, and in 1901, to counter Baldwin, several smaller locomotive builders, including Schenectady and Brooks, joined forces to form the American Locomotive Company, commonly known as "Alco." The same year, the Lima Locomotive and Machine Company of Lima, Ohio—which had built the geared Shay type since 1880—was reorganized as the Lima Locomotive Works to build conventional locomotives. In the first half of the twentieth century, Baldwin, Alco, and Lima were the most significant commercial builders in the United States. Several eastern railroads—notably, the Pennsylvania and the Norfolk & Western—also designed and constructed large numbers of their own locomotives. Several significant builders of smaller industrial and switching locomotives were also located in the East, including the Climax Manufacturing Company in Corry, Pennsylvania; Vulcan Iron Works in Wilkes-Barre, Pennsylvania; and H. K. Porter Company of Pittsburgh.

Various railroads, preservation groups, historical societies, and private organizations have made main-line steam trips a reality in the East, enabling some of the largest preserved locomotives to work the main lines again. The Reading Company operated its T-1 4-8-4s on Reading Rambles beginning in the late 1950s. Starting in the 1960s, the Southern Railway organized trips on its lines, and both the Southern and its successor, Norfolk Southern (NS), have operated locomotives on trips over its lines, including the Norfolk & Western's famous J-class No. 611 and A-class No. 1218. Although, the NS's steam program concluded in 1994, operation of the engines allowed thousands of people to experience big steam decades after revenue operations had ended.

In the 1980s, the famous Pennsylvania Railroad Class K4s Pacific No. 1361 was removed from its perch at the Horseshoe Curve, restored to operating condition, and briefly resurrected. Elsewhere, the Chesapeake & Ohio's massive 4-8-4 No. 614 has made many outings, while railroads such as the New York, Susquehanna & Western and the Reading & Northern have operated steam trips over their lines.

Main-line steam trips, however, have been relatively rare occurrences in the East. The best place to experience steam is at one of the many tourist railways or railroad museums that focus on steam preservation. In New England, the Conway Scenic Railway in New Hampshire and the Valley Railroad in Connecticut have regularly operated steam for several decades. The state of Pennsylvania hosts some of America's finest historic lines and museums, including the Strasburg Rail Road and the Railroad Museum of Pennsylvania at Strasburg; the Steamtown National Historic Site in Scranton; the East Broad Top Railroad at Orbisonia; and the Wanamaker, Kempton & Southern at Kempton, among others. Farther south, in Maryland, the Baltimore & Ohio Railroad Museum and the Western Maryland Scenic Railroad are worth the trip.

Previous pages:
Southern Railway No. 4501 works between St. Matthews and Branchville, South Carolina, on September 4, 1970. This handsome Mikado was so popular that it was the sole topic of a book by late *Trains* magazine editor David P. Morgan. *George W. Kowanski*

The first American-built steam locomotive made its public debut on August 28, 1830. Constructed by New York industrialist Peter Cooper to demonstrate to the Baltimore & Ohio the ability of American industry to produce working locomotives, this machine successfully hauled 13 tons at 4 miles per hour. *Brian Solomon*

Left: Unlike most railroad locomotives, Peter Cooper's employed a vertical boiler derived from marine practice. Because of its small size, this curious machine was compared with a popular circus figure named Tom Thumb, and the name stuck. The B&O's 1927 replica weighs roughly 7 tons compared with Cooper's original, estimated to weigh only 1 ton. *Brian Solomon*

Above: In the formative days of American railroading, Peter Cooper's locomotive led to a distinctive design first built by Phineas Davis and later by Ross Winans. Ultimately, this design died out in favor of more successful designs based on Robert Stephenson's famous *Rocket.* On November 9, 1996, B&O successor CSX borrowed the 1927-built replica for show on the original B&O main line at Ellicott City, Maryland. *Brian Solomon*

Above: Horatio Allen, one of America's railroad pioneers, earned a reputation on Pennsylvania's Delaware & Hudson in the 1820s. He made history by importing British-made locomotives to work the line. Although unsuccessful in that effort, he soon moved to the South Carolina Railroad, where he ordered a pioneering American-designed locomotive called the *Best Friend of Charleston. George W. Kowanski*

Opposite top: South Carolina Railroad's *Best Friend of Charleston* was designed by E. L. Miller of Charleston and constructed at the West Point Foundry in New York City. It was delivered in autumn 1830. In June 1831, *Best Friend* was destroyed by a boiler explosion. This 1928-built replica was posed with Southern Railway No. 722 at Charleston in 1970 to mark the South Carolina Railroad's 140th anniversary. *George W. Kowanski*

Opposite bottom: On January 15, 1831, *Best Friend* became the first American locomotive to haul a regularly scheduled passenger train. The replica is owned by the city of Charleston. As of 2008, the locomotive was on loan to South Carolina Railroad successor Norfolk Southern and displayed at the company's offices in Atlanta, Georgia. *George W. Kowanski*

The Norfolk & Western is remembered for retaining big steam power longer than any other major railroad in the United States. Its late-era designs were among the finest steam locomotives to work American rails. N&W's Roanoke Shops turned out 14 well-crafted J-class 4-8-4s that set performance and reliability records. In one test run, a J reached 110 miles per hour with a 15-car 1,025-ton train. In service, the 4-8-4s turned 15,000 miles per month. *Brian Solomon*

Above: Long ago eclipsed by its famous sister, Norfolk & Western J No. 610 is serviced at Schafer's Crossing in Roanoke, Virginia, on July 31, 1958. N&W's sleek, modern, J-class locomotives were routinely assigned to the railroad's finest long-distance passenger runs, including the *Pocahontas* and the *Powhatan Arrow. Richard Jay Solomon*

Left: In the 1980s, the Norfolk & Western restored No. 611 to active service, and it became a regular star of steam excursions. In August 1994, No. 611 races toward the setting sun west of Valparaiso, Indiana, on one of its final excursion runs for Norfolk Southern. After more than a decade of excursions, the streamliner was returned to the Virginia Museum of Transportation at Roanoke. Its boiler has been cold ever since. *Brian Solomon*

Retired in 1959, N&W No. 611 was preserved at the Virginia Museum of Transportation, making it one of only a handful of streamlined steam locomotives to escape scrapping. In 1982, Norfolk Southern restored No. 611 to service, and for the next dozen years it operated numerous excursions across the NS system. Here, it works westward at Eggleston, Virginia. *George W. Kowanski*

Left: Along with J-class No. 611, another star of Norfolk Southern's steam program was A class No. 1218. On August 1, 1987, NS choreographed operation of these two locomotives on its former N&W main line west of Roanoke at Christiansburg, Virginia. *George W. Kowanski*

Above: Bathed in its own smoke and steam, N&W No. 611 charges west at Hardy, West Virginia, on October 23, 1982. In their day, the N&W's J-class locomotives were noted as exceptionally smooth-running machines. Precision counterbalancing helped minimize destructive dynamic forces. *George W. Kowanski*

The star of Western Maryland Scenic's popular excursion service is No. 734, a locomotive typical of the large-boiler 2-8-0 Consolidation types once common in freight service in the United States. *Brian Solomon*

Left: Western Maryland Scenic Railroad operates the old Western Maryland Railroad grade west of Cumberland, Maryland, to Frostburg. Here, No. 734 works upgrade at Helmstetter's Curve. *Brian Solomon*

Above: No. 734 was built by Alco and labored in ore service on the Lake Superior & Ishpeming in Michigan's Upper Peninsula. Today, it is dressed as a Western Maryland locomotive for excursion service. *Brian Solomon*

The Southern Railway concluded regular steam operations in 1953, but No. 4501 wasn't among the last steam to work in revenue service on the Southern. It had been sold to the Kentucky & Tennessee Railway back in 1948. In 1964, the Tennessee Valley Railroad Museum restored the old Mikado, and in 1966 it began working main-line excursions on old home rails. Here, No. 4501 is surrounded by adoring fans at Salisbury, North Carolina, on August 25, 1966. *John Gruber*

Above: Baldwin built Southern No. 4501 in 1911. The Southern's Ms-class ("s" for "superheating") Mikados were handsome, nicely proportioned, and powerful locomotives but otherwise unremarkable in their day. The Southern revived No. 4501 and made it a star of its steam program, where it entertained tens of thousands of people in two decades of main-line excursions. Working the Seaboard Coast Line rails in 1970, No. 4501 heads southward at Yemassee, South Carolina. *George W. Kowanski*

Left: On September 4, 1970, Southern Railway No. 4501, with a National Railway Historical Society–sponsored excursion from Washington, D.C., to Charleston, South Carolina, pauses at Columbia. On the locomotive's pilot is the Southern's president, W. Graham Claytor, who was instrumental in putting the locomotive in main-line excursion service. In 1982, Ronald Reagan appointed Claytor to run Amtrak. *George W. Kowanski*

Right: After the Reading's regular steam operations were discontinued, it assigned three of its Class T-1 4-8-4s to "Reading Ramble" excursion service on lines in eastern Pennsylvania. Nos. 2100 and 2102 lead an excursion in October 1964. *Richard Jay Solomon*

Above: Working west on the Central Railroad of New Jersey, Reading No. 2102 passes Netherwood, New Jersey, in 1972. A popular excursion locomotive for decades, No. 2102 has resided in recent years on the Blue Mountain & Reading/Reading & Northern, which operates former Reading Company routes in Pennsylvania. *George W. Kowanski*

During 1945 and 1947, when most lines were ordering new diesels, the Reading Company constructed 30 4-8-4s using boiler components from retired 2-8-0 Consolidations. No. 2102 was photographed in February 1972 at Hampton, New Jersey, while on an excursion over the Central Railroad of New Jersey from Elizabeth, New Jersey, to Bethlehem, Pennsylvania. *George W. Kowanski*

Right: On a locomotive, the valve gear serves a function similar to that of a transmission on an automobile. Consisting of rods, eccentrics, and links, the valve gear allows the engineer to control the position of the valves that direct the flow of the steam to the cylinders, thus adjusting the power and direction of the engine. Baker valve gear, seen here on C&O No. 614, was one of several patented arrangements used on select late-era steam locomotives. *Brian Solomon*

Above: An excursion train led by Chesapeake & Ohio Greenbrier No. 614 rolls eastward across Moodna Viaduct at Salisbury Mills, on its way from Port Jervis, New York, to Hoboken, New Jersey. This massive former–Erie Railroad viaduct takes its name from Moodna Creek, which runs through the valley. *Brian Solomon*

Chesapeake & Ohio No. 614 works east on the former Erie main line at S curves near Tuxedo, New York. This magnificent machine was one of five that Lima built for the coal-hauling C&O in 1948. On the C&O, 4-8-4s were known as Greenbriers, named for the Greenbrier River. Where some railroads ordered 4-8-4s for freight, the C&O's were designed for heavy passenger service. *Brian Solomon*

The C&O continued buying new steam locomotives after World War II, when most lines were buying only diesels. C&O J-3a No. 614 charges through Tuxedo, New York, with more than 20 passenger cars in tow in June 1997. *Brian Solomon*

Above: By 1948, few railroads were ordering new steam, which made the C&O's Greenbriers something of a novelty in postwar motive power and among the last 4-8-4s built in the United States. In September 1980, C&O No. 614 ascends Baltimore & Ohio's famous 17-Mile Grade at Bond, Maryland. *George W. Kowanski*

Left: The C&O's final Greenbriers were considered very modern, featuring roller bearings on all axles and side rods, aluminum cabs and boiler jacketing, and other late-era equipment and accessories. *Brian Solomon*

Right: Typically, Lima builder's plates were diamond shaped, while Baldwin's were circular and Alco's rectangular. This difference made it relatively easy to tell the builder of big steam without the need to study the fine print. *Brian Solomon*

Above: Chesapeake & Ohio No. 614 was one powerful set of wheels. With 72-inch wheels and 27 1/2×30-inch cylinders, and operating with 255 psi boiler pressure, this machine could get up and go. In June 1997, No. 614 makes a show of it at Port Jervis, New York. *Brian Solomon*

A low headlight and a high bell were typical of most C&O late-era steam power. Mechanically, the C&O's J-3a 4-8-4s were near cousins to the Nickel Plate Road's S-class Berkshires. Working an excursion train on the former Erie Graham Line, No. 614 pounds the rails near Salisbury Mills, New York. *Brian Solomon*

Right: The stainless-steel trim, headlight, and number board on Chesapeake & Ohio Class L-1 4-6-4 No. 490 typified the popular art deco styling of the period. The reign of the C&O's streamlined Hudson was pretty short, ending when the railroad bought Electro-Motive E-units in 1951. *Brian Solomon*

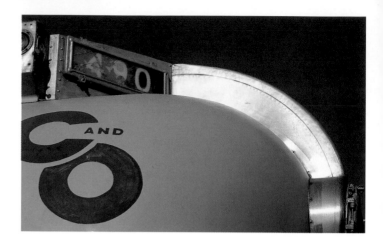

Above: C&O No. 490 works the main line in Kentucky on July 2, 1947. Today, this is one of only a few preserved Hudson types in the United States. *J. R. Quinn collection*

Early locomotive streamlining was intended to reduce wind resistance and thus improve fuel consumption. Later attempts were largely to make locomotives seem modern. *Brian Solomon*

Above: No. 65 has been a popular attraction since the Wanamaker, Kempton & Southern acquired it from Safe Harbor Water Power Corporation in 1970. This handsome saddle-tank type is characteristic of small industrial switch engines found all across North America. Here, it captures the essence of rural railroading while working up a short grade south of Wanamaker, Pennsylvania, on a former Reading Company branch line. *Brian Solomon*

Right: Steam railroading at night is a visceral experience: the distractions of daytime are subdued, accentuating the machine's sounds and aromas, and allowing its power to resonate in the soul. Wanamaker, Kempton & Southern No. 65 is bathed in its own steam at the Kempton, Pennsylvania, station after finishing its "Harvest Moon" special run to Wanamaker. *Brian Solomon*

No. 65 was a 0-6-0T built by H. K. Porter Company of Pittsburgh and sold in 1930 to the Safe Harbor Water Power Corporation, which used it in construction of the Safe Harbor dam along the Susquehanna River. Unlike larger locomotive manufacturers such as Baldwin and Alco that built customized designs to meet individual railroad specifications, Porter specialized in manufacturing stock-designed, small- to moderate-sized industrial locomotives. *Brian Solomon*

Pioneer Tunnel Coal Mine No. 1 is maintained to haul short excursions on this industrial railway at Ashland, Pennsylvania. On a humid summer morning, crewmembers douse hot cinders dumped from the firebox. Vulcan Iron Works was one of several locomotive builders in Pennsylvania. Vulcan built more than 4,000 locomotives between 1874 and 1950, focusing its production on small industrial types such as this 0-4-0T. *Brian Solomon*

Above: The Pioneer Colliery was opened in 1853 and closed in 1931. After 1873, the mine was part of the Reading Company empire. The line was rebuilt as a tourist attraction that provides views of the Mahanoy Mountains and old open-pit coal mines. Tracks are narrow compared with the main line—just 42 inches between the flanges. Pioneer Tunnel Coal Mine locomotive No. 1 is named after politician Henry Clay. *Brian Solomon*

Left: Instead of more modern piston valves, Pioneer Tunnel Coal Mine locomotive No. 1 uses traditional slide valves, easily identified by the boxy appendage above the cylinder. Small cylinders and tiny drive wheels are sufficient for moving coal jennies from the mine. *Brian Solomon*

Above: Middletown & Hummelstown is a Pennsylvania short line operating a few miles of former Reading Company trackage. It runs seasonal passenger excursions using diesels and this well-preserved former Canadian National 2-6-0. Locomotives with six-coupled driving wheels and a leading, pivoting two-wheeled pony truck came on the North American scene about 1860. Compared with the tiny 4-4-0 locomotives of the period, the 2-6-0 arrangement seemed enormous and so these locomotives were called Moguls. *Brian Solomon*

Right: The M&H's former Canadian National 2-6-0 Mogul type is a nicely balanced machine akin to No. 89, which works nearby on the Strasburg Rail Road (see pages 44–45). *Brian Solomon*

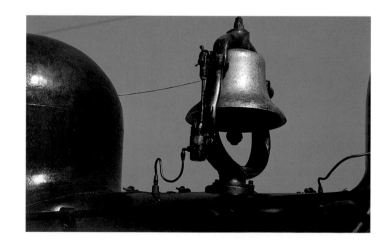

Fresh from a recent overhaul, M&H No. 91 eases out of the shop at Middletown, Pennsylvania, in September 2008. The original M&H was a 6 1/2-mile line chartered in 1888; the present M&H short line began on the eve of Conrail in 1976. *Brian Solomon*

Though the 2-6-0 Mogul type once seemed enormous, old Canadian National No. 89, working at Strasburg, Pennsylvania, today seems tiny compared with the much larger locomotives displayed across the road at the Railroad Museum of Pennsylvania. *Brian Solomon*

Above: No. 89 crosses cornfields on the return leg of an autumn afternoon excursion. Most of the year, the Strasburg Rail Road provides steam-hauled excursions in Pennsylvania Dutch country, making it one of the region's most loved tourist railways. *Brian Solomon*

Left: No. 89 was built in 1910 by the Canadian Locomotive Company for the Grand Trunk Railway. After the GT was melded into the Canadian National Railway in the 1920s, the locomotive served the CNR. Today, it is one of several steam locomotives on the Strasburg Rail Road. *Brian Solomon*

Right: Strasburg Rail Road 2-10-0 No. 90's 56-inch-diameter drivers pound the rails at Strasburg, Pennsylvania. Freight locomotives typically had smaller wheels than those designed for passenger service. Smaller wheels make starting tonnage freights easier, while taller wheels are more effective for operating at higher speeds. *Brian Solomon*

Above: The Strasburg is one of the few railroads in Pennsylvania where steam locomotives operate a regular schedule on a daily basis. *Brian Solomon*

No. 90 has just arrived at the East Strasburg, Pennsylvania, station. This handsome Decapod type was built by Baldwin in 1924 for the Great Western Railway in Loveland, Colorado. In its day as a freight hauler, it moved train loads of sugar beets. It has operated on the Strasburg since 1967. *Brian Solomon*

Above: Popular with enthusiasts, Strasburg No. 475 is not universally liked by crews because of its cramped cab. It has worked at the Strasburg Rail Road since its restoration in 1993. *Brian Solomon*

Right: Norfolk & Western No. 475 once hauled both freight and passenger trains in rural Virginia. Its 21×30-inch cylinders power 56-inch driving wheels. *Brian Solomon*

The 4-8-0 Twelve-Wheeler was not a common type, and the Norfolk & Western had one of the largest rosters in the United States. Old N&W M-class No. 475 was built by Baldwin in 1906 and served in both freight and passenger service for the better part of a half century. On this brisk November afternoon, Strasburg No. 475 approaches the Blackhorse Road crossing at Carpenters on its return run from Lehman Place. *Brian Solomon*

Right: Built by the Grand Trunk's Point St. Charles Shops in April 1921, this classic 0-6-0 switcher was on the Canadian National roster until 1959. (The Grand Trunk became a component of the Canadian National system in 1923.) Since 1971, it has been at North Conway, New Hampshire, where it works on the Conway Scenic Railway. *Brian Solomon*

Above: No. 7470 goes for a spin on the North Conway, New Hampshire, turntable. This locomotive has regularly worked excursions on the Conway Scenic Railway's former Boston & Maine and Maine Central lines in New Hampshire's White Mountains. *Brian Solomon*

Built by the thousands, the 0-6-0 switcher was one of the most common steam locomotives in North America. Typically used for switching freight and passenger cars, the ordinary yard goat didn't attract much attention in the days of steam, but today the Conway Scenic's 0-6-0 No. 7470 is regularly assigned passenger excursions. *Brian Solomon*

Above: Locomotive No. 40 was built by Alco in 1920 for the Portland, Astoria & Pacific. It was briefly owned by the Southern Pacific before going to North Carolina's Aberdine & Rockfish, where it worked for many years. It arrived on Connecticut's Valley Railroad in 1977 and has been entertaining visitors there for three decades. *Brian Solomon*

Right: The 2-8-2 Mikado was based on the successful 2-8-0 Consolidation and 2-6-2 Prairie types. The combination of eight drivers with a comparatively large firebox made it ideal for moving freights, and it became the most popular type of road steam locomotive built in twentieth-century America. *Brian Solomon*

A view down the length of the locomotive from the tender. No. 40's relatively small-diameter drive wheels were typical of branch-line freight locomotives, where traction is more important than speed. *Brian Solomon*

Above: No. 40's conductor guides the engineer using hand signals at Essex, Connecticut. The throttle is open, and with the hiss of steam escaping from cylinders, the engine is just beginning to move. *Brian Solomon*

Right: Brilliant fall foliage makes the Valley Railroad a pleasant seasonal excursion. On its morning run, No. 40 works from Essex toward Deep River. Built as an oil-burner, No. 40 was converted to coal-fired operation in the 1930s. *Brian Solomon*

Morning at Essex, Connecticut, evokes the atmosphere of a small New England station more than 60 years ago. Here, the crew prepares for its run as locomotive No. 40 simmers near the platform. *Brian Solomon*

No. 26 receives nominal maintenance at Steamtown's former Lackawanna Scranton roundhouse. This classic 0-6-0 switcher was built by locomotive manufacturer Baldwin for its own use as a shop switcher. It is one of several locomotives that Steamtown has restored to working order. *Brian Solomon*

Left: The crosshead guides the piston thrust while connecting the piston with the main rod, used to turn the driving wheels. A number of different types of crossheads have been applied over the years. This style, known as the "alligator," was introduced circa 1880. The secondary crosshead connection is part of the valve gear. *Brian Solomon*

Above: No. 26 was constructed in March 1929 for use at Baldwin Locomotive Works' then-recently expanded Eddystone, Pennsylvania, plant. In 1948, Baldwin sold the locomotive to the Jackson Iron and Steel Company in Jackson, Ohio, where it remained through the 1970s. It was acquired by Steamtown in 1986, arriving on the property in Scranton in 1990. The 0-6-0 is one of the most common steam locomotive types preserved in the United States. *George W. Kowanski*

With the Delaware & Hudson's Bernie O'Brien at the throttle, Canadian Pacific No. 2317 charges upgrade with a Steamtown excursion at Hallstead, Pennsylvania. This CPR Class G-3-c Pacific type was built by Montreal Locomotive Works in June 1923 and served for 36 years. It was among the locomotives acquired by the late F. Nelson Blount that have become the core of the Steamtown collection. *George W. Kowanski*

Left: As a regular engine for Steamtown excursions, No. 2317 is familiar to the site's many visitors. Here, the fireman gives a friendly wave on a rainy October day in downtown Scranton. *Brian Solomon*

Above: In July 1995, an evening lineup at Steamtown's former Lackawanna roundhouse finds no fewer than five locomotives under steam. From left to right: Baldwin 0-6-0 No. 26, Canadian National Mikado No. 3254, Canadian Pacific Railway No. 2317, and two visiting locomotives, Blue Mountain & Reading (former Gulf Mobile & Northern) Pacific No. 425 and Lowville & Beaver River Railroad Shay No 8. *George W. Kowanski*

Above: Among the most exciting displays at Scranton's Steamtown National Historic Site are live steam locomotives. In recent years, a regular performer has been Canadian National Mikado No. 3254, which often hauls the demonstration excursion train. *Brian Solomon*

Right: The fireman leans out of the cab of No. 3254 to get a better view along the boiler. Built by the Canadian Locomotive Company at its Kingston (Ontario) Works in 1917, this locomotive originally served the Canadian National's predecessor, the Canadian Government Railways. *Brian Solomon*

Steamtown acquired No. 3254 in 1987 through a trade with the Gettysburg Railroad for Canadian Pacific 4-6-2 No. 1278, which was one of several operable steam locomotives when Steamtown was located at Bellows Falls, Vermont. The collection was moved to Scranton in 1984.
Brian Solomon

Right: East Broad Top No. 12 is the oldest and smallest of the road's Mikado fleet. It is known on the railroad as *Millie.* *Brian Solomon*

Above: Between 1911 and 1920, the coal-hauling East Broad Top made the unusual step of buying a new fleet of narrow gauge locomotives consisting of six Baldwin Mikados of various sizes. Here, Mikado No. 12 doubleheads with No. 15 on an autumn excursion from Orbisonia to Colgate Grove. *Brian Solomon*

The narrow gauge East Broad Top built south from a connection with the Pennsylvania Railroad at Mt. Union. In August 1873, the EBT reached Orbisonia, 11 miles from Mt. Union. To tap the Broad Top coal fields, the railroad built farther south, reaching Robertsdale in October 1874. By the mid-1950s, its coal traffic had tapped out, and in 1956 the line was abandoned. The railroad was bought by a scrapper that preserved it rather than ripping it up. *Brian Solomon*

Above: East Broad Top Nos. 14 and 15 were built to the same specifications and are 17 tons heavier and slightly more powerful than *Millie* (see pages 62–63), yet smaller than the railroad's heaviest Mikados, Nos. 16, 17 (see pages 66–67), and 18. *Brian Solomon*

Right: Compared with American main lines, which are 4 feet 8 1/2 inches between the rails, the East Broad Top's rails are just 3 feet apart. No. 15 leads an evening excursion downgrade toward Orbisonia. The region's rural charm, combined with the East Broad Top's well-preserved antique railway equipment, has made the railroad a popular attraction since the 1960s. *Brian Solomon*

Leading the first train over the line in nearly a week, No. 15 polishes rusty rails as it works the grade south of Orbisonia on a chilly autumn morning. The sights and sounds of the East Broad Top transport visitors back 80 years to when steam locomotives ruled Pennsylvania's rails. *Brian Solomon*

Above: No. 17 is one of the last Mikados built for the East Broad Top and one of the largest on the line. It was capable of hauling 22 steel hoppers with roughly 700 tons of coal up the ruling northbound grade from the mines to Mt. Union. While Nos. 16 and 18 have been cold since the railroad ended common carrier operations in the 1950s, No. 17 made occasional appearances through the 1990s. *Brian Solomon*

Right: The East Broad Top's once-profitable common carrier operations ended in 1956, but a few miles of line were reopened for excursion service in 1960. The railroad occasionally operates freight excursions for the benefit of visitors. Here, No. 17 is fired up for the annual Fall Spectacular. *Brian Solomon*

East Broad Top No. 17 is one of the only surviving locomotives in the United States equipped with the unusual Southern valve-gear arrangement. *Brian Solomon*

On August 4, 1987, Norfolk & Western A-class No. 1218 plies home rails at Bluefield, West Virginia. The N&W A-class were 2-6-6-4 simple articulated types (high-pressure steam to all cylinders) designed for relatively fast running and equipped with roller bearings on all axles. With two sets of cylinders and running gear beneath one boiler, an articulated locomotive effectively comprises two engines worked from a common throttle. *George W. Kowanski*

Left: The N&W concluded heavy steam operations in 1960, several years later than on most American railroads. In the 1980s, No. 1218 was restored to working order, and on August 1, 1987, as part of the National Railroad Historical Society convention, it hauled a train of empty coal hoppers for the delight of photographers.
George W. Kowanski

Above: No. 1218 leads an excursion down 19th Street in Erie, Pennsylvania. The N&W was one of only a few railroads to build its own steam locomotives in the twentieth century. No. 1218 was built in 1943 by the railroad's Roanoke Shops. *Brian Solomon*

Above: The Pennsylvania Railroad's K4s Pacific type was built as a passenger locomotive and became one of the most recognized steam locomotives of its day. For three decades, No. 1361 was displayed at Horseshoe Curve. In 1985, it was removed from its perch and briefly restored to working order. On August 27, 1988, the locomotive emerges from the Howard Tunnel on the old Pennsy Northern Central route. *George W. Kowanski*

Opposite top: To celebrate York's 150th anniversary of railroading, No. 1361 operated seven roundtrips from York, Pennsylvania, to Hanover Junction and Menges Mills between August 26 and 28, 1988. *George W. Kowanski*

Opposite bottom: In 1914, the Pennsylvania Railroad introduced its first Class K4s Pacific. This design was a fusion of the PRR's experimental K29s Pacific and its excellent E6s Atlantic. The K4s proved to be the best passenger locomotive the railroad ever built. The type was mass-produced beginning in 1917, sharing its boiler and other key components with the PRR's L1s Mikado. *George W. Kowanski*

The Pennsylvania Railroad's E2s Atlantics were fast machines. In March 1904, No. 7002 made a special speed run with the PRR claiming it reached 127.1 miles per hour—a record not universally accepted. The PRR scrapped the original 7002 in 1934 and later dressed up another member of the same class, No. 8063, to represent the famous runner. The Railroad Museum of Pennsylvania's second 7002 was operated for a few years in excursion service on the Strasburg Rail Road. *George W. Kowanski*

Left: Although fast, the Atlantic type fell out of favor early because it lacked power to move the longer and heavier trains that emerged with the advent of all-steel passenger cars after 1910. Only a handful of Atlantics have been preserved. Although the second No. 7002 made outings on the Strasburg Rail Road and worked main-line excursions during the 1980s, it is now a static display inside the Railroad Museum of Pennsylvania. *Brian Solomon*

Above: Built by the Pennsylvania Railroad's Juniata Shops at Altoona in 1905, this classic Atlantic type has been dressed with all the period adornment associated with early twentieth-century passenger steam. Note the gold-painted trim on the wheels and tender. In later years, the PRR's locomotives exhibited a more spartan appearance. *George W. Kowanski*

Chapter 2
Trains Across the Plains

Trains Across the Plains

Railroads enabled the rapid settlement and development of the Midwest, where relatively level terrain allowed numerous lines to crisscross the region with relative ease. Locomotive whistles echoing across the cornfields became routine sounds in daily life. Some towns in Ohio, Indiana, and Illinois were served by numerous railway lines that typically crossed each other at grade. Important gateway cities emerged where lines met to interchange freight and where passengers changed trains. The greatest of these gateways was Chicago, which became known as America's railroad capital because of the large numbers of railroads that met there.

Eastern lines, including the Pennsylvania Railroad, New York Central, and Baltimore & Ohio, extended lines to reach Chicago, Cincinnati, and St. Louis. The Nickel Plate Road reached from Buffalo via Cleveland to Chicago and St. Louis. Other railroads began at Chicago and were built westward. Of these, the Santa Fe and the Milwaukee Road ultimately reached the West Coast. Other lines, such as the Chicago & North Western, the Rock Island, and the Burlington, were content to serve the central region.

In the mid-nineteenth century, the 4-4-0 American type developed as the most popular locomotive in North America. As railroads grew busier, the need to haul longer and heavier freight trains and faster and heavier passenger trains spurred locomotive development. New types were developed, both for freight and passenger service, including the 2-6-0 Mogul, which had a greater number of drive wheels than the American type and therefore was better suited for freight. Later, the Mogul became an ideal type for light branch work, serving both freight and passenger trains. The 2-8-0 Consolidation emerged as a standard freight locomotive, built in large numbers during the late nineteenth century and early twentieth century. It was succeeded by the 2-8-2 Mikado, which became the most popular freight locomotive after about 1910.

Passenger locomotives were built more for speed than for hauling heavy tonnage. The 4-6-0 Ten-Wheeler was based on the 4-4-0 American, as was the 4-4-2 Atlantic, with its substantially larger firebox. The 4-6-2 Pacific melded the best of the 4-6-0 and the Atlantic types, and was the most popular passenger steam locomotive of the twentieth century. Some Midwestern railroads were partial to the 2-6-2 Prairie, a type well suited to light lines and level running.

Evermore massive locomotives were built after 1910. Articulated types using two sets of drive wheels on frame that bends laterally, thereby allowing numerous drivers under one boiler to negotiate tight curvature, were desirable on mountain lines and in territory where extremely heavy freights were operated. Although used by some Midwestern lines, articulated types were less common in the Midwest than in the mountains of the East and West.

In the 1920s, the quest for power and speed led to the development of superpower steam. Ohio's Lima Locomotive Works was the pioneer of superpower. While the 2-8-4 Berkshire type was first built for use on the Boston & Albany, several Midwestern railroads, including the Illinois Central and the Nickel Plate Road, were famous for their Berkshires. The 4-6-4 Hudson was developed as a superpower passenger locomotive. The type was used on many lines in the Midwest, including the New York Central, which operated the locomotives to Chicago and St. Louis on its famous passenger trains. The Santa Fe, Burlington, Milwaukee Road, and Canadian Pacific were also known for their Hudsons. A more popular superpower type and one widely embraced all over the United States and by Canadian National—the largest owner of the type—was the 4-8-4. Although often called the Northern type, many railroads objected to this name. The 4-8-4 was well suited to fast freight and fast passenger operations. Relative to the Hudson, which is rare in preservation, a large number of 4-8-4s survived into the diesel age, and several have been used on main-line steam trips in modern times.

There is a great legacy of preserved steam in the central states. A host of museums and preserved lines have displayed and operated steam there, and main-line steam excursions have been relatively common and very popular. In the last 20 years, Milwaukee Road's No. 261, Cotton Belt No. 819, and Union Pacific No. 844—all 4-8-4 types—have been regular visitors on lines in the central part of the country.

Previous pages:
The Nickel Plate Road (NKP) was among the last American railroads to order new steam locomotives and also one of the last to operate large steam in Midwest road-freight service. Several Nickel Plate locomotives have been preserved and operated in main-line excursion service. On May 7, 1980, NKP Berkshire No. 765 worked a freight train on the Toledo, Peoria & Western. *George W. Kowanski*

Above: Milwaukee Road Class S-3 No. 261 is a powerful Northern type built during World War II when the War Production Board limited diesel production and encouraged railroads to acquire new steam power. Minneapolis-based North Star Rail Corporation, in cooperation with The Friends of the 261, regularly operates No. 261 in main-line excursion service. *Brian Solomon*

Right: Milwaukee Road No. 261 works west along the Mississippi River near Savanna, Illinois. The railroad bought its first 4-8-4 in 1930—a Baldwin designed for passenger service. The Milwaukee Road's final order for 4-8-4s was for 10 Alco-built war babies, including No. 261, acquired in 1944 for both freight and passenger service.
Brian Solomon

One of the best seats in railroading is the fireman's position aboard a large steam locomotive.
Brian Solomon

Above: All of the Lackawanna's famous 4-8-4 Poconos were scrapped, so when Steamtown National Historic Site in Scranton, Pennsylvania, wanted to re-create a Pocono for a promotional film, it borrowed Milwaukee Road No. 261 and dressed it up as Lackawanna No. 1661. En route to Pennsylvania on October 11, 1994, the disguised locomotive rolls through Waukesha, Wisconsin, on the Wisconsin Central. *Brian Solomon*

Right: No. 261 makes a run for Milwaukee in the evening twilight. For many years, No. 261 sat as a static display at the National Railroad Museum in Green Bay, Wisconsin, before it was leased and restored by the North Star Rail Corporation in the early 1990s.
Brian Solomon

Heading toward Chicago Union Station on old home rails, Milwaukee Road No. 261 accelerates away from A2 Tower in June 2004. *Brian Solomon*

The first rays of daylight catch Northern Pacific No. 328 under steam at Dresser, Wisconsin, in August 1996. The large horizontal tank above the cylinders and running gear is the air reservoir used for the Westinghouse automatic airbrake. *Brian Solomon*

Above: The Ten-Wheeler type was first built in the 1840s but gained in popularity after the 1860s. Long after the perfection of larger types, this wheel arrangement continued to be built as a dual-service locomotive. Northern Pacific No. 328, built in 1905, is a classic example of a versatile early twentieth-century locomotive. *Brian Solomon*

Left: The first rays of sun illuminate Northern Pacific No. 328's exhaust steam as it tows a wooden-sided Soo Line caboose around the wye at Dresser, Wisconsin, on August 17, 1996. *Brian Solomon*

Above: Northern Pacific Class S-10 No. 328 has 57-inch driving wheels that are more or less typical for a locomotive its size. Curiously, this machine was built for the South Manchurian Railway but sold by Alco's Rogers Works to the Northern Pacific in 1907. *Brian Solomon*

Right: A classic Alco-order sand dome sits atop the boiler on Northern Pacific No. 328. This locomotive was restored to operating condition in 1981 and worked for two decades as an excursion engine for the Minnesota Transportation Museum. *Brian Solomon*

As strange as it might seem today, traditional steam-era operating practice only saw headlights switched on when it was dark. *Brian Solomon*

Soo Line No. 1003 was built by Alco in 1913 and enjoyed a remarkably long career. It was retired in 1954 as the railroad was completing its dieselization but was kept in standby service until 1959. On December 17, 2007, the engineer of No. 1003 guides the locomotive on former Milwaukee Road trackage north of Random Lake, Wisconsin. *Chris Guss*

Above: In the 1960s and 1970s, Soo Line No. 1003 was displayed in a park at Superior, Wisconsin. Briefly steamed in the early 1980s, the Class L-1 2-8-2 Mikado was returned to active service in 1996 following an extensive restoration. In a scene that was commonplace across North America more than 60 years ago, No. 1003 passes through the heart of Fredonia, Wisconsin. *Chris Guss*

Left: No. 1003 is one of several serviceable standard gauge Mikados in the United States. Dozens of enthusiasts were on hand to follow No. 1003 on its leisurely jaunt from Plymouth, Wisconsin, on December 15, 2007. The slowly falling snow en route gave the chase a surreal quality, muting most of the landscape surrounding the train and letting the mind wander back to a day when steam ruled the land. *Chris Guss*

This Chinese Mikado was the last steam locomotive in the world to roll off a regular assembly line. In 1988, it was sold new to Iowa's Boone & Scenic Valley. Like all steam locomotives, it never fails to capture the enthusiasm of observers. *Brian Solomon*

Above: Boone & Scenic Valley No. JS8419 undergoes its routine morning blow-down procedure on the high trestle west of Boone, Iowa. Blow down is necessary to remove mineral accumulation in the boiler. In the summer, the Boone & Scenic Valley runs weekend trips with the locomotive on its former interurban trackage along the Des Moines River in central Iowa. *Brian Solomon*

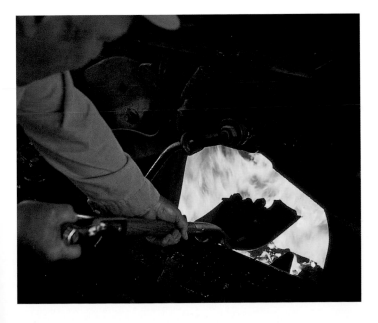

Left: A fireman's job is to maintain the fire aboard the locomotive. Although the Boone & Scenic Valley's Chinese Mikado has a mechanical stoker, it is rarely used because the trains are relatively light and there are no challenging grades on the line. *Brian Solomon*

Above: Mikado No. 14 was built by Baldwin in 1913 for the Duluth & Northern Minnesota. In its early years, it worked at Knife River, Minnesota, and was later sold to the Lake Superior & Ishpeming. Since 1981, it has belonged to the Lake Superior Transportation Museum. In July 1996, the locomotive works on the North Shore Scenic Railroad with an excursion toward Two Harbors. *Brian Solomon*

Right: Rods transmit the power of the pistons to the drive wheels, thus converting lateral motion to rotary motion. *Brian Solomon*

No. 14 is bathed in its own steam on an abnormally cool July evening at Duluth after its run to Two Harbors. The locomotive operated in excursion service for several years and last worked in 1998. Today, it is a static display. *Brian Solomon*

This 1901-built Baldwin 2-6-2 once worked for the McCloud River Railroad in California. It is seen here in 1996 on Wisconsin's Kettle Moraine Railway, a popular excursion line operated on a light, isolated, former Milwaukee Road branch line. Sadly, suburban sprawl caught up with the railway and hostility from unsympathetic neighbors was among the reasons for its closing in autumn 2001. The locomotive was donated to the National Railroad Museum at Green Bay, Wisconsin.
Brian Solomon

Above: The 2-6-2 Prairie type was introduced as a main-line freight locomotive and was briefly tried as a fast passenger engine. Later, it found a niche as a lightweight, branch-line locomotive. The wheel arrangement got its name because of its early popularity with Midwestern granger lines. *Brian Solomon*

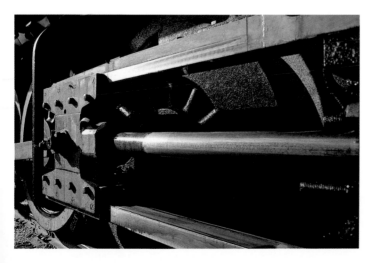

Left: Detail of the crosshead and lead driving wheel on the Kettle Moraine Railway No. 9. *Brian Solomon*

The Class R-1 Ten-Wheeler best represents Chicago & North Western (C&NW) steam. In its day, the R-1 was the most common and most versatile type on the railroad. No. 1385 was built by Alco in 1907 and during its long tenure handled a great variety of freight and passenger trains. On a frosty February afternoon, No. 1385 waits at North Freedom, Wisconsin, for the arrival of Saginaw Timber No. 2. *Brian Solomon*

Three C&NW R-1s escaped scrapping. One is preserved at the Forney Transportation Museum in Colorado, and another is privately owned and stored in Upper Michigan. The best known of the three, however, is No. 1385, which resides at the Mid-Continent Railway Museum at North Freedom, Wisconsin. It was operated for a number of years to the thrill of visitors but has been stored since 1998.
Brian Solomon

The old Delaware, Lackawanna & Western never owned a Ten-Wheeler numbered 1061, although it owned a number of Alco-built 4-6-0s in that number series. In 1994, C&NW No. 1385 posed as DL&W 4-6-0 No. 1053 for a Steamtown promotional film.
Brian Solomon

On frigid February 18, 1996, Saginaw Timber Company No. 2 takes on water at North Freedom, Wisconsin. Steam locomotives required lots of water. To keep boilers full, line-side tanks were located at strategic points. *Brian Solomon*

No. 2 is seen through the North Freedom station window. The 2-8-2 Mikado type was developed as a popular freight locomotive in the first decades of the twentieth century. This Baldwin from 1912 was first used by the Saginaw Timber Company and later served a variety of small railroads, including the Polson Lumber Company. In the 1980s, the Mid-Continent Railway Museum restored it to its as-built appearance. *Brian Solomon*

No. 2 makes for a silhouette of steel in a cloud of its own exhaust steam. In the 1990s, the Mid-Continent Railway Museum was blessed with two fine operating steam locomotives. Since 2000, No. 2 has been cold, and now excursions are operated with diesels. Because steam has undeniable appeal for visitors, the museum began raising funds for the restoration of its steam locomotives. *Brian Solomon*

On an overcast afternoon in spring 1968, Nickel Plate Road (NKP) No. 759 leads an excursion near Albany, New York. The 2-8-4 configuration was developed in the mid-1920s by Will Woodard of Lima Locomotive Works for the New York Central's Boston & Albany line, which coined the Berkshire name in honor of the mountains in western Massachusetts. *Richard Jay Solomon*

Above: In the late 1960s and early 1970s, NKP No. 759 was restored to service and operated many public excursions. It even hauled a few freight trains on the Erie Lackawanna and the Western Maryland. On September 12, 1970, it roared west at Newport, Pennsylvania, on the Penn Central's four-track former Pennsylvania Railroad Main Line. Today, No. 759 is a static display at Steamtown in Scranton, Pennsylvania. *George W. Kowanski*

Left: The Nickel Plate Road connected Buffalo and Cleveland with Chicago and St. Louis. The railroad was among the last in the East to work big steam in freight service. However, the railroad barely survived the steam era and in 1964 lost its identity when it was bought by the Norfolk & Western. Today, former Nickel Plate lines are operated by Norfolk Southern, one of the largest railway companies in the East. *Richard Jay Solomon*

The intense traffic demands of World War II placed the Nickel Plate—like all American railroads—in a power crunch. In 1942 and 1943, Lima built 25 Berkshires based on the design of the NKP's S-class 2-8-4s that were built in 1934. Another 30 followed in 1944—in fact, all wartime 2-8-4s were the NKP's Class S-2. After the war, while most lines were buying diesels, the Nickel Plate bucked the trend and bought 10 more Class S-3 Berkshires, built by Lima in 1949. No. 765 is operated by the Fort Wayne (Indiana) Historical Society. *Brian Solomon*

No. 765 works Conrail's multiple-track Niagara Branch near Black Rock, New York. The Berkshire type was the first superpower locomotive, a distinct improvement over earlier designs. The type was built to efficiently haul more freight faster than any previous type. The success of the Berkshire, with its enlarged firebox and boiler, led to a host of new superpower designs. *Brian Solomon*

The first Berkshires that served the Boston & Albany were mountain climbers equipped with driving wheels measuring 63 inches in diameter. By contrast, the Nickel Plate's Berkshires were built for speed and featured 69-inch driving wheels. *Brian Solomon*

Nickel Plate Road No. 765 marches through Black Rock in Buffalo, New York, on July 2, 1989.
Brian Solomon

Above: In May 1980, No. 765 makes a show on the Toledo, Peoria & Western at East Peoria, Illinois. Fort Wayne Historical Society's No. 765 operated main-line excursions for many years and completed a thorough restoration in 2005. *George W. Kowanski*

Left: On May 7, 1980, No. 765 shows that it still can do what it was built for as it hauls Toledo, Peoria & Western tonnage across the Illinois Central diamonds at Gilman, Illinois.
George W. Kowanski

In the 1940s and 1950s, the Duluth, Missabe & Iron Range operated enormous Yellowstone articulated types in heavy iron-ore service. DM&IR No. 225 is displayed in a park near DM&IR Proctor Yard in Proctor, Minnesota. *Brian Solomon*

Above: In 1928, the Northern Pacific was the first to adopt the 2-8-8-4 simple articulated locomotive, which it called the Yellowstone type. These were the largest locomotives in the world at the time. The Duluth, Missabe & Iron Range operated a fleet of 18 Baldwin-built Yellowstones. *Brian Solomon*

Left: A street sign in the mining town of Mountain Iron on Minnesota's Iron Range. The DM&IR bought its Yellowstone fleet between 1941 and 1943. They operated as late as 1960, and three have been preserved. *Brian Solomon*

Above: Among the Southern Pacific's affiliated railways was the St. Louis Southwestern, known by its nickname, the Cotton Belt. In October 1988, enthusiasts gather around in admiration of Cotton Belt 4-8-4 No. 819 at Tyler, Texas, with an excursion from Pine Bluff, Arkansas. The Cotton Belt's Class L-1 4-8-4s were built by the railroad's Pine Bluff Shops. *Lewis Raby, courtesy of Tom Kline*

Opposite top: No. 819 storms westward past vintage searchlight signals at Gilmer, Texas, leading an excursion train heading to Tyler, Texas, for the annual Tyler Rose Festival, on October 15, 1993. This magnificent 4-8-4 is maintained in operable condition at Pine Bluff, Arkansas, but has not made main-line trips in recent years. *Tom Kline*

Opposite bottom: Cotton Belt No. 819 charges through the rain on home rails at Buena Vista, Arkansas, on October 16, 1992. This World War II–era locomotive was near 50 years old at the time of the photograph and yet was still capable of maintaining passenger-train speeds. *Tom Kline*

Above: Frisco No. 1522 is a 4-8-2 Mountain type, a wheel arrangement first built in 1911 for passenger service on the Chesapeake & Ohio. The type was later widely adopted across North America for both freight and passenger applications. On September 28, 2002, No. 1522 is seen east of Eureka, Missouri. *Chris Guss*

Right: Working as the star attraction on the Burlington Northern Santa Fe's *Employee Appreciation Special* in May 2001, old Frisco No. 1522 carries a BNSF flag above the markers. The St. Louis & San Francisco was absorbed by the Burlington Northern in 1980, decades after it dumped the fires on its last steam locomotives.
Tom Kline

Working east at the end of the day, Frisco No. 1522 is east of Newberg, Missouri. *Chris Guss*

The Southern Pacific, including its lines in Mexico, operated a total of 164 2-8-2 Mikados, a relatively small number considering the size of the railroad. By comparison, it had far larger fleets of 2-6-0, 4-6-0, and 2-8-0 types. Of its Mikados, five were set aside for preservation, including No. 786, which sat on display at Austin, Texas, for years until its restoration in 1991. *Tom Kline*

No. 786 was built by Alco at the former Brooks Locomotive Works in Dunkirk, New York, in 1916 and is representative of the Southern Pacific Mikados, featuring 63-inch driving wheels and 200-psi boiler pressure. Mikados were workhorse locomotives. Although often assigned to freight, some worked passenger trains, especially this engine, which spent its years on the railroad's Texas and Louisiana lines. *Tom Kline*

On a clear but frigid winter morning, engineer Joe Dale Morris, who at the time was the general manager of the Austin Steam Train Association, looks back from the cab of Southern Pacific No. 786 to inspect his train at Bertram, Texas, on November 22, 1992. The train, known as the *Hill Country Flyer*, operates between Cedar Park (near Austin) and Burnett, Texas, on a former SP line that was purchased by the city of Austin. *Tom Kline*

Chapter 3
Taming the West

Taming the West

Railroads in the West followed a distinct developmental pattern different from that of the rest of the country. While railroads in the East tended to connect existing communities and serve industry, the early lines in the West were built across hundreds of miles of unsettled and undeveloped land, and required large federal subsidies to encourage and finance construction. Light population densities and vast distances resulted in fewer lines than elsewhere in the country. Except for a few established locations, such as Denver, Salt Lake City, and San Francisco, many western communities owe their founding to the coming of the railroad.

Western railroads were built to handle transcontinental traffic, serve regional agriculture (including the cattle and timber trades), and tap mineral resources. A handful of large railroads dominated the scene, but there were dozens of smaller lines.

Geographical characteristics of western lines affected locomotive development in a variety of ways. Western railroads tended to be heavily graded, often with steep, prolonged climbs. As a result, railroads sought evermore powerful machines. In the nineteenth century, the Central Pacific/Southern Pacific pushed the limits of design by building and buying a significant number of 4-8-0 Twelve-Wheelers and manufacturing the only known 4-10-0 in a failed effort to increase power. Between 1902 and 1904, the Santa Fe expanded the 2-10-0 Decapod by adding trailing trucks, resulting in the 2-10-2 Santa Fe type. (The Southern Pacific bought large numbers of 2-10-2s in the 1910s and 1920s but refused to acknowledge the name of their competitor, referring to the type as "Decks.")

Various specialized articulated types were common on western lines, and the Great Northern was the first to buy articulated Mallet (named for Swiss mechanical engineer Anatole Mallet, and pronounced "mallay") compounds for road service, ordering 2-6-6-2s from Baldwin in 1906. (The first North American railroad to use the Mallet was the Baltimore & Ohio, which two years earlier had adapted it as a helper locomotive.) For better service on Donner Pass, where smoke was a problem in snow sheds and long tunnels, the Southern Pacific reversed the articulated type, moving the cab forward.

Other railroads built some of the largest steam locomotives in the world to handle greater amounts of tonnage. The largest in the West was the Union Pacific's 4-8-8-4 Big Boy of 1941, a type expanded from the already enormous 4-6-6-4 Challenger.

Not all of the West's giant steam locomotives were articulated types, however. In the 1920s, the Union Pacific had originated the 4-10-2 Overland type and expanded this locomotive to the 4-12-2 Union Pacific type, featuring the longest rigid wheelbase of any locomotive ever constructed. The Northern Pacific was first to adopt the 4-8-4, which it called the Northern type, while another articulated type, the 2-10-4, was known as the Texas type.

Among the other distinctive characteristics of many western railroads was the choice of fuel. From the late nineteenth century onward, most railroads in the East burned coal. The dearth of accessible coal on the other side of the continent, however, led to the development of oil-burning steam locomotives in the far West. The Santa Fe pioneered the oil-burner, and by the first decades of the twentieth century, most railroads on the West Coast were using oil-burning steam locomotives.

The crucial role of the railroad in developing the West has played an important part in locomotive preservation. Western communities have been well aware of the importance of the steam locomotive, and in the 1950s, western railroads were exceptionally generous in donating examples of their locomotives to towns and cities along their lines. While a great many smaller locomotives—0-6-0s, 2-8-0s, and the like—found their way into town parks, a number of larger machines were preserved. The Southern Pacific's famous No. 4449 was displayed for a number of years in a city park in Portland, Oregon, before being restored to service in the mid-1970s for the American Freedom Train. The Union Pacific not only preserved many of its locomotives, but also retained some for its own use. No. 844, for example, was never dropped from the roster and has continued to run since it was built in 1944.

The popularity of the Rio Grande narrow gauge resulted in one of America's first tourist railways, the Durango & Silverton, and contributed to the preservation in 1970 of the Antonito, Colorado–to–Chama, New Mexico, segment of the Rio Grande as the Cumbres & Toltec Scenic Railroad. Both lines operate with former Rio Grande 2-8-2 Mikados.

Previous pages:
The Rio Grande's narrow gauge Silverton Branch was built to tap mine traffic. The railroad tried to abandon the line in the 1950s, but interest in its steam-hauled passenger trains spurred a revival as a tourist hauler. The growth in passenger ridership proved profitable, and the Rio Grande began to promote steam trains as a tourist attraction. Brightly painted passenger cars and an Old West theme were used to attract visitors. Former Rio Grande Class K-36 No. 482 leads an excursion northward through Beaver Creek Canyon, Colorado, in September 1995. *Tom Kline*

Southern Pacific No. 4449, a streamlined 4-8-4 Class GS-4 built by Lima, has become one of the most famous locomotives in America. In 1991, it worked an excursion to Railfair Sacramento from Portland, Oregon. Here, the locomotive works hard at Ericson, California, with a long consist of *Daylight*-painted passenger cars in tow. *Brian Solomon*

Left: The stylized *Daylight* insignia was designed by Charles L. Eggleston and introduced in 1937 for SP's new streamlined trains between San Francisco and Los Angeles. The *Daylight* scheme incorporated colors associated with California. *Daylight* orange is a near match to the hue of the California poppy, while the golden connotation harks back to the gold rush. *Tom Kline*

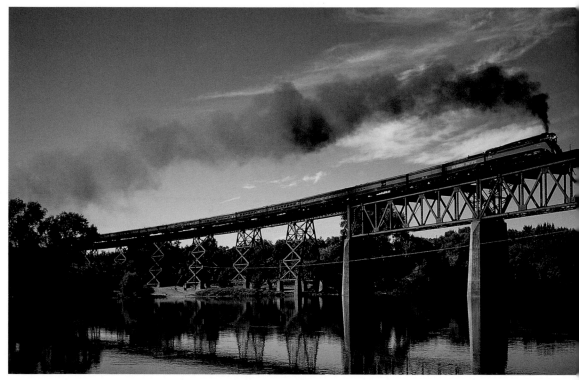

Above: The GS-4 was the zenith of the Southern Pacific's Northern types. In 1941, Lima built 28 of them—Nos. 4430 to 4457. Of these, only No. 4449 survives. Here, No. 4449 leads an excursion across the Sacramento River at Redding, California. *Brian Solomon*

In May 1991, Southern Pacific No. 4449 leads an eastward excursion along the shore of San Pablo Bay near Pinole, California. In the Southern Pacific classification system, 4-8-4 types were classified "GS," for "general service" or "Golden State." *Brian Solomon*

Looking much like it did back in the 1940s, No. 4449 works upgrade on home rails at Worden, Oregon, on its way to Sacramento on April 28, 1991.
Brian Solomon

Although impressive when observed from a distance, the enormous size of a steam locomotive is most evident when you get up close. No. 4449 rests at Redding, California, before making a run to Black Butte and back.
Brian Solomon

Southern Pacific No. 4449 was one of three steam locomotives recruited to haul the American Freedom Train, a patriotic exercise designed to coincide with the American Bicentennial in 1976. The train carried historical artifacts and toured the continental United States for millions to see. *George W. Kowanski*

Left: Streamlined No. 4449 awes young observers. When styling the *Daylight*, the Southern Pacific left no detail untouched. Even elements such as the pilot were given the *Daylight* treatment. *Brian Solomon*

Above: Two generations of Southern Pacific passenger steam: On the left is Baldwin-built P-8 Pacific-type No. 2472, one of 15 locomotives delivered in 1921; on the right is No. 4449, built in 1941. When new, both types represented the best of the railroad's passenger power. Today, these classics inspire nostalgia for passenger trains that once connected California cities with those across the southwestern United States. *Brian Solomon*

In spring 1991, the Southern Pacific's Class P-8 No. 2472 and GS-4 No. 4449 lead a Railfair Sacramento excursion along the shore of San Pablo Bay at Pinole, California. *Brian Solomon*

This detail of No. 2472 shows the crosshead, main rod, valve gear, and driving wheels. Part of the attraction of steam locomotives is that the majority of the operating equipment is out in the open for all to see. *Brian Solomon*

No. 2472 is a Class P-8 Pacific type built by Baldwin in 1921. Like many twentieth-century Southern Pacific steam locomotives, it's an oil-burner. *Brian Solomon*

Popular with railway enthusiasts, No. 2472 made an extended visit to the Niles Canyon Railway in 2008. In this view, it pulls an excursion train toward Sunol, California. *Brian Solomon*

Above: In August 1992, restored No. 2472 leads an eastward excursion on the Coast Line near Harlem, California. This handsome locomotive has thrilled thousands in excursion service since 1991 and is one of a few active Pacific types in the United States. *Brian Solomon*

Left: The SP's Pacific types were standard main-line passenger power in the 1920s and 1930s. The P-8s survived to the end of steam, working in secondary services, and were retired in the 1950s. In April 1991, No. 2472 is seen at Oakland's Jack London Square on its maiden run following restoration. *Brian Solomon*

Right: No. 3 was built by Lima in 1912 for the Alaculsy Lumber Company in Tennessee. In 1945, it worked for the Coal Processing Corporation at Dixiana, Virginia, from which it got its name. Since 1962, No. 3 has served as a tourist locomotive at the Roaring Camp & Big Trees at Felton, California, where it brings visitors over a re-created narrow gauge logging railroad. *Brian Solomon*

Above: Built in the 1960s, California's Roaring Camp & Big Trees emulates steeply graded, timber-hauling, narrow gauge lines common in California in the early twentieth century. Grades reach 10 percent—a rise of 10 feet for every 100 traveled—impossibly steep for conventional steam locomotives but easily conquered by geared steam. *Brian Solomon*

Conventional reciprocating rod–driven steam locomotives were ineffective for industrial applications, where poor track, steep grades, and slow operating speeds were the norm. Filling this gap were steam locomotives with geared drives, the most popular of which was the Shay type, named for its designer, lumberman Ephraim Shay, and built by Lima. Roaring Camp & Big Trees No. 3, named *Dixiana*, is typical of a two-truck Shay used in lumber service. *Brian Solomon*

Above: No. 28 is a handsome 2-8-0 Consolidation type built by Baldwin in 1922 for the Sierra Railway. When No. 28 eases out of the yard at Jamestown, California, it's doing so on home rails. Except for infrequent displays in Sacramento, old No. 28 has never worked off line. *Brian Solomon*

Right: Before a day of excursion work, Sierra Railway No. 28 comes up to pressure inside the railway's vintage 1910 roundhouse, one of the last in the western United States. Today, the historic Sierra Railway—a part of Railtown 1897, managed by the California State Railroad Museum—operates seasonal weekend steam and diesel excursions using trackage rights on 3 miles of Sierra Railroad. *Brian Solomon*

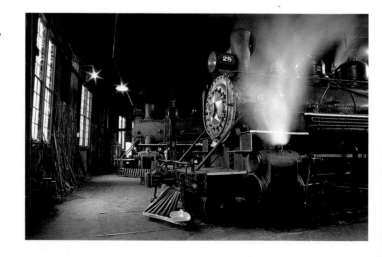

The Sierra Railway has been a choice location for film and television for decades, and old No. 28 has starred in several productions. Yet, this 2-8-0 is not an exceptional machine, but rather typical of moderately sized locomotives of its period. *Brian Solomon*

No. 18 has had an unusual history. It left the Baldwin Locomotive Works in 1912 for the McCloud River Railroad, where it worked until 1956. Its revenue freight work behind it, the Mikado was sold to the nearby Yreka Western short line for a brief excursion service career that ended in the early 1960s. In 1998, the McCloud bought the locomotive back, restoring it to service in 2001, only to sell it a few years later. It's seen here in March 2008, operating a trip on the Sierra Railroad out of Oakdale, California. *John Gruber*

Above: McCloud River Railroad Baldwin Mikado No. 18 is coupled with the Sierra Railroad's S12 Baldwin switcher No. 42 at Oakdale, California. *John Gruber*

This Baldwin 2-6-0 Mogul type was built by Baldwin for the Southern Pacific in 1901. At the time of its construction, compounding was a popular system for reducing operating costs, and No. 1744 was among a number of SP locomotives built as a four-cylinder Vauclain compound, in which high-pressure cylinders exhausted into low-pressure cylinders to make double use of the steam. The savings proved illusory, as high maintenance costs canceled out efficiency gains. No. 1744, along with many other compounds, was rebuilt as the conventional simple engine pictured here. *George W. Kowanski*

In the 1980s, No. 1744 was a regular excursion engine on the Heber Creeper, a tourist railway operating on a former Rio Grande standard gauge branch in Utah. In 2008, the tourist line was known as the Heber Valley Railroad, while No. 1744 was working excursions on another former Rio Grande line hundreds of miles away. *George W. Kowanski*

Earl Knoob replaces a burned-out lamp on No. 1744, working in Rio Grande Scenic Railroad excursion service on the San Luis & Rio Grande. This classic Mogul was one of two steam locomotives used to haul trains up the standard gauge La Veta Pass in recent years. *Tom Kline*

Above: No. 346 was built in July 1881 by Baldwin for the Denver & Rio Grande Railway, a predecessor of what would become the Denver & Rio Grande Western Railroad. Originally, it was numbered 406 and named *Cumbres*. It is preserved in working order at the Colorado Railroad Museum at Golden. *Brian Solomon*

Right: While most of the operable Rio Grande narrow gauge steam locomotives are twentieth-century 2-8-2 Mikados, No. 346 is a 2-8-0 and is a generation older than the earliest narrow gauge Mikados. It had nearly a half century of operation by the time the last D&RGW Mikados were delivered. *Brian Solomon*

In 1870, the Denver & Rio Grande's William Jackson Palmer sailed to Great Britain for an extended honeymoon. There, he inspected the 2-foot-gauge slate-hauling Festiniog Railway in North Wales and met leading narrow gauge proponents who advised Palmer to adopt narrow gauge. The Rio Grande's first locomotive was a 2-4-0, but it soon adopted larger types. *Brian Solomon*

Above: The Rio Grande's K-27s—popularly known as "Mudhens"—were the first locomotives built with outside frames, along with outside counterweights and crankpins. No. 463 works as a helper ahead of a K-36 with a train that has just reached the summit of Cumbres Pass, Colorado, on the Cumbres & Toltec Scenic Railroad. *Brian Solomon*

Right: Mudhens were the smallest of the D&RG's Mikados, yet were considered enormous by narrow gauge standards of the day. No. 463 is under steam at Chama, New Mexico. *Brian Solomon*

The Cumbres & Toltec Scenic Railroad's heavy excursion trains require a helper from Chama, New Mexico, up the 4 percent grade to Cumbres Pass. No. 463 is a head-end helper that has paused at Cresco tank for water. Before World War I, the Denver & Rio Grande upgraded the west slope of Cumbres Pass with heavier track to permit operation of K-27s as helpers. *Brian Solomon*

Right: Most of the Denver & Rio Grande Western's twentieth-century narrow gauge steam locomotives were Baldwin products. The exceptions were the 10 Class K-28 Mikados built by Alco in 1923. Known popularly as "Sport Models," these locomotives—including No. 478—were regularly assigned to passenger trains. No. 478 leads a Durango & Silverton excursion at Silverton, Colorado. *Brian Solomon*

Above: During World War II, seven D&RGW K-28s were sent to the White Pass & Yukon in Alaska, where they served for a short time. After the war, they were scrapped. The three surviving K-28s now operate on the Durango & Silverton. A pair of K-28s doublehead on a northward excursion train in Colorado's Animas River Canyon in 1995. *Tom Kline*

No. 478 at Durango, Colorado, August 1991. D&RGW's Silverton Branch traffic had largely tapped out by the 1950s, but tourist ridership was profitable, so the line evolved into one of the first modern tourist railways. The line was later sold off, creating the Durango & Silverton. *Brian Solomon*

In 1925, the Denver & Rio Grande Western ordered an additional 10 outside-frame Class K-36 Mikados from Baldwin. The Rio Grande's K-36 Mikados were the last all-new narrow gauge locomotives built for the railroad. *Tom Kline*

Above: No. 481 leads an excursion on a narrow shelf high above the Animas River. Each of the Rio Grande's four classes of narrow gauge Mikados featured a distinct number sequence. The K-27s were numbered in the 450s and 460s, K-28s in the 470s, K-36s in the 480s, and K-37s in the 490s. *Brian Solomon*

Left: No. 481 leads a returning excursion toward Durango, Colorado, on a clear summer afternoon. *Brian Solomon*

Above: A mechanic attaches a blue flag to Durango & Silverton No. 482. The blue flag is the most restrictive signal on a railroad. It prevents a piece of equipment from being moved, and the signal can only be removed by the employee who places it. *Tom Kline*

Opposite top: Alco-built K-28 No. 478 and Baldwin K-36 No. 482 rest at Silverton, Colorado, after making their run along the Animas River from Durango. At one time, Silverton was an important railway hub where mining lines fed the Denver & Rio Grande Western. Today, it's the end of the line. *Tom Kline*

Opposite bottom: No. 482 catches the sun as it climbs through Pinkerton, Colorado, on September 20, 1995. The Durango & Silverton is among the most popular excursion railways in the West. *Tom Kline*

The Cumbres & Toltec Scenic Railroad operates an excursion line using the former Denver & Rio Grande Western San Juan extension between Antonito, Colorado, and Chama, New Mexico. Here, C&TS K-36 No. 487 works the grade over Cumbres Pass, one of the highest remaining lines in North America. *Brian Solomon*

Cumbres & Toltec's former Rio Grande No. 487 carries a removable plow. Beneath the plow is a more typical pilot such as that seen on sister K-36 No. 481 (see pages 140–141). *Brian Solomon*

After a day's service, the fireman and engineer of No. 487 converse in the cab at Chama, New Mexico. The locomotive was built in 1925. In 1970, it was conveyed, along with 64 miles of former Rio Grande trackage, to the Cumbres & Toltec Scenic Railroad, which is jointly owned by the states of Colorado and New Mexico. *Brian Solomon*

To permit a significantly larger and more powerful narrow gauge locomotive, the Rio Grande's Mikados required a specialized design featuring outside frames, crankpins, and counterweights instead of the arrangement typical of standard gauge locomotives. Introduced with K-27s in 1903, this design was last applied to the K-37s that the railroad rebuilt from standard gauge 2-8-0s between 1928 and 1930. *Brian Solomon*

Above: Rio Grande K-37 No. 497 leads a Cumbres & Toltec photo freight near Big Horn, New Mexico, in September 1999. After years of decline, Rio Grande abandoned its San Juan extension in 1969. By that time, freight operations had become sporadic and the railroad had greatly deteriorated. The exceptionally scenic 64-mile section along the Toltec Gorge and over Cumbres Pass was preserved by the states of Colorado and New Mexico as the Cumbres & Toltec Scenic Railroad. While C&TS typically operates passenger excursions, occasionally it runs period freights for photographers. *Tom Kline*

Left: No. 497 works from Chama to the summit at Cumbres Pass. This grueling climb is one of the best places to find steam locomotives working in North America.
Brian Solomon

The locomotive *Sonoma*, engine No. 12, is a classic wood-burner adorned in the style typical of engines built in the mid-Victorian period. Polished Russian iron boiler plate, ornate brass fittings, and detailed paintwork were among the trademarks of this period. In the 1930s, it was recognized as an antique gem and set aside for preservation. Today, it is beautifully restored and displayed at the California State Railroad Museum in Sacramento. *Brian Solomon*

No. 12 is a nicely proportioned narrow gauge 4-4-0 American type built by Baldwin in 1876 for California's North Pacific Coast, a railway built to connect ferry piers at Sausalito with timber stands along the Russian River Valley. After a few years, it was sold and spent most of its operating life on the Nevada Central Railway. Today, it is beautifully restored and displayed at the California State Railroad Museum in Sacramento. *Brian Solomon*

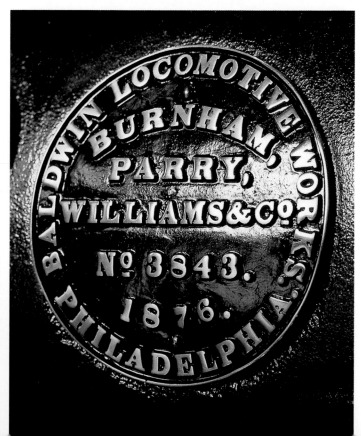

Baldwin builder's plate on the North Pacific Coast's No. 12. *Brian Solomon*

Above: The Eureka & Palisade's No. 4 *Eureka* is a classic 3-foot-gauge 4-4-0 built by Baldwin in July 1875. For years, this beautiful locomotive was owned by Warner Bros. for use in motion pictures. Today, it is privately owned and usually stored near Las Vegas, Nevada. *Tom Kline*

Right: No. 4 has made an occasional appearance on the Durango & Silverton. A lightweight compared with the massive machines of the twentieth century, No. 4 weighs just 22 1/2 tons—almost 1/17 the weight of a Union Pacific Big Boy. *Tom Kline*

The *Eureka* is a near cousin to the *Sonoma* preserved at the California State Railroad Museum (see pages 148–149). Both 4-4-0s were built as wood-burners and lushly adorned in the ornate style of the period. *Tom Kline*

The Union Pacific's 800 4-8-4s were fast and powerful engines designed to operate with a 1,000-ton passenger train at a sustained 90 miles per hour. Union Pacific No. 844—the last in its class—not only escaped retirement, but has operated nearly every year since it rolled out of Alco's Schenectady, New York, plant in 1944. In August 1996, it worked east to Chicago over the former Chicago & North Western main line. *Brian Solomon*

Left: Today, No. 844 is one of very few American steam locomotives still owned and operated by the railroad that bought it. In September 1989, it took a break from excursion service to haul a grain train to Cheyenne, Wyoming. It is pictured here climbing Archer Hill. *Brian Solomon*

Above: During the years when the Union Pacific had GP30 No. 844, its preserved 4-8-4 carried an extra "4." In April 1981, Union Pacific Nos. 8444 and 3985 lead an excursion over the Southern Pacific's Donner Pass on their way to Railfair Sacramento. The train has just exited Tunnel No. 7 and is about to enter Tunnel No. 6 at Donner Summit. The trackage here was part of the original 1868 Donner crossing, built as part of the first transcontinental railroad. *George W. Kowanski*

Union Pacific No. 3985 leads an excursion to San Jose over Altamont Pass in 1992. The UP's 4-6-6-4 Challengers were among the most successful high-speed articulated types, combining the benefits of a four-wheel leading truck and tall driving wheels with contemporary innovations for better stability at higher speeds. *Brian Solomon*

The Union Pacific's Bob Krieger holds No. 3985's engineer's seat during a switching move. This popular locomotive has operated in excursion service across the UP's vast western network. *Tom Kline*

The Union Pacific's Challengers were designed for speeds of 70 miles per hour. These huge, powerful machines offered operational flexibility as a result of articulation and exceptional power. As of 2008, No. 3985 was the largest operating locomotive in the world. *Brian Solomon*

Union Pacific No. 3985 leads an excursion eastward at Peru, Wyoming, on June 28, 1982. The Challenger type was designed by the Union Pacific's assistant general superintendent Otto Jablemann. The first of the type was built by Alco in 1936. Built in 1943, No. 3985 was part of the final order for the type. *George W. Kowanski*

Left: Fireman Rick Braunschweig has his hand on the injector lever and his eye on the sight glass as water fills No. 3985's enormous boiler at Trinity, Texas, in June 2004. *Tom Kline*

Above: Under sunny skies on June 14, 1993, No. 3985 and DDA40X No. 6936 climb eastward at Quartz with the *Oregon Trail Special*. Eastern Oregon is famous for its heavily graded UP main line. This is the west slope of Encina Hill, just a few miles east of Baker City. In the distance are the snow-crested peaks of the Blue Mountains. *Brian Solomon*

Chapter 4
Steam in Europe

Steam in Europe

The locomotive developed differently in Britain than it did in North America. The more restrictive loading gauge in Britain required more compact locomotive design. Not only did British steam locomotives tend to be smaller, lower, and shorter than their American counterparts, they appeared neater because various appliances and equipment were kept within tighter confines. British steam locomotives were built with inside cylinders and inside valve gear decades after this style was abandoned in North America. Outside valve gear, common in America after 1910, was not widely adopted by British designs for another generation. Further, American locomotives were largely free from extraneous adornment after about 1885, but British locomotives continued to feature decorative trappings until the 1940s.

Most of Britain's railways were grouped into the "Big Four" companies in 1923. The London, Midland & Scottish Railway, the Great Western Railway, the London & North Eastern Railway, and the Southern Railway were regional systems that operated the bulk of the British railway network until

the system was nationalized in 1947. British Railways, as the unified system was called, stuck with steam a decade longer than its U.S. counterparts. Britain's last steam locomotive, *Evening Star*, was built in 1960—the same year main-line steam operations ended in the United States. Main-line steam in Britain continued until 1968.

Britain has recognized its steam legacy and today offers some of the world's finest preserved railways with dozens of locomotives kept in working order. The great variety of preserved railways allows visitors to experience many types of locomotives working in diverse settings and applications. The Great Central Railway in Leicestershire has rebuilt a section of former main line, including a significant portion of double track. There, several locomotives may be working the line at one time, creating an aura of big-time operations reminiscent of the 1950s when steam ruled British rails. The Severn Valley Railway (SVR) has re-created the atmosphere of a secondary line, featuring several small stations and operating through its bucolic, namesake valley. In season, this 16-mile-long railway operates a regular passenger service that connects at Kidderminster with main-line passenger services. It is not unusual to find five or more locomotives under steam on the SVR. Of a similar concept, although not as extensive, is the Keighley & Worth Valley, a 5-mile line that connects its namesake points and retains all the flavor of a British branch line.

Wales is famous for its narrow gauge railways, of which the Festiniog is the best known. This former slate-hauling line uses tracks just 1 foot 11 1/2 inches wide and operates a number of classic locomotives, including articulated Fairlie types. Affiliated with the Festiniog is the Welsh Highland Railway that operates Garratt locomotives, a type never used in the United States. Instead of the conventional rigid frame and the boiler riding atop the running gear, a Garratt type features a boiler suspended on the frame between two sets of articulated running gear, thus enabling the use of a large boiler on a narrow gauge locomotive.

Ireland's railways were built by British engineers in the Victorian period and used locomotives either built by British manufacturers or largely influenced by British designs. Unlike railways in Britain, North America, and most of continental Europe, Ireland's railways are largely broad gauge— 5 feet 3 inches between the rails. Ireland began buying large numbers of diesel-electric locomotives in the 1950s, and by 1963 the conversion from steam power was complete. Today, the Railway Preservation Society of Ireland routinely operates main-line excursions with historic steam locomotives over both the Irish Rail and the Northern Ireland Railways.

Steam power may be experienced in a number of countries on the European continent. Among regular operations are Austria's narrow gauge Zillertalbahn, operating between Jenbach and Mayrhofen, and Polish National Railways, known for maintaining the last standard gauge steam roundhouse in Europe in daily operation. Also noteworthy are several narrow gauge steam operations in Germany, where standard gauge steam is occasionally used for main-line excursions. In addition, steam-hauled trains are sometimes used for regular services in what Germans refer to as plandampfs, or "timetabled steam."

Previous pages:
The quiet fields of County Wexford in Ireland are momentarily disturbed by the puff-puff-puff of Great Southern & Western Railway No. 186 as it slowly climbs Taylorstown bank between Wellingtonbridge and Ballycullane on its way to Waterford. *Brian Solomon*

Under a good head of steam, the West Country Pacific type *Boscastle* leads an excursion on Britain's preserved Great Central Railway in Leicestershire. The Southern Railway had 66 West Country Pacifics. *Brian Solomon*

Above: Between 1923 and 1947, Britain's Southern Railway operated most of the lines south of London. Southern chief mechanical officer O. V. S. Bulleid had worked under Sir Nigel Gresley on the London North Eastern Railway and continued to refine Gresley's concepts on the Southern's Pacific types in the 1940s. Bulleid's West Country light Pacifics were introduced in 1945. Locomotive No. 34039 *Boscastle* is a modified West Country type that has had much of its original streamlined shrouding removed. *Brian Solomon*

Left: The West Country Pacifics have a similar appearance to Bulleid's Merchant Navy class. Both were considered compact machines compared with those built for American railroads. They were just 12 feet 11 inches tall and 67 feet 4 3/4 inches long, including the tender. By contrast, a Pennsylvania Railroad K4s Pacific measured 74 feet 8 inches long. *Brian Solomon*

Marching upgrade in heavy rain, the Southern Railway's West Country Pacific No. 21C123, *Blackmoor Vale*, leads an excursion on the Bluebell Railway. This preserved line south of London operates 9 miles of a former Southern Railway secondary main line that was trimmed from the network in the 1960s. *Brian Solomon*

Left: Blackmoor Vale looks very much the way the West Country Pacific class appeared when new back in 1945. It features the full streamlining treatment and is painted in the Southern's Malachite green. Here, it approaches Horsted Keynes on the preserved Bluebell Railway. *Brian Solomon*

Above: Blackmoor Vale was one of many British steam locomotives rescued from a scrapper in South Wales during the 1960s and 1970s. Operational British steam survived on a wider scale much later than in America, but the transition to other modes was more rapid. The last revenue steam disappeared in August 1968. *Brian Solomon*

The London, Midland & Scottish Railway's chief mechanical officer, W. A. Stanier, was well known for his exceptionally good locomotive designs. His Class 5 4-6-0, popularly known as the Black Five, was the most numerous locomotive type built in twentieth-century Britain. Preserved Black Five No. 45110 passes mechanically operated semaphores at Bewdley on Britain's Severn Valley Railway. *Brian Solomon*

Dressed in the British Railways' livery of the 1950s, Black Five No. 45110 works on the Severn Valley Railway. The Black Five was introduced in Britain the same year that the Burlington's diesel-powered *Zephyr* made its debut in America. The *Zephyr* was retired in 1960 after spawning widespread interest in dieselization, while Britain built its last steam locomotive that same year. Some of the Black Fives worked right to the end of steam in 1968. *Brian Solomon*

The 4-6-0 was a popular type on the London, Midland & Scottish Railway prior to the design of the Black Five in 1934. When LMS was formed in 1923, it inherited more than 800 4-6-0s from predecessor companies. The success of Stanier's Black Five not only led to mass production, but made it the platform for British Rail's 5MT design built from 1951 to 1957. *Brian Solomon*

Best known of the Great Western Railway's 4-6-0s was its celebrated King class capable of sustained high-speed running. By contrast, No. 7812, *Erlestoke Manor*, is an example of the GWR's Manor class, a type derived from the Grange class 4-6-0 and specifically for use on lighter lines. No. 7812 approaches Bewdley on a former GWR line preserved by the Severn Valley Railway. *Brian Solomon*

No. 7812 pauses with an excursion train at Arley on the Severn Valley Railway, a preserved line more than 16 miles long that is home to a variety of restored steam locomotives. Arley is one of several active stations on the line that retain the character of an age gone by.
Brian Solomon

Driving wheels of No. 7812, *Erlestoke Manor*, one of three GWR Manor class 4-6-0s preserved on the Severn Valley Railway. Thirty of this class were built between 1930 and 1950. Relatively light axle weight with good pulling characteristics made them ideal for passenger service on lightly built secondary lines. This locomotive dates to 1939. *Brian Solomon*

Above: From 1923 until nationalization of British Railways in 1947, the London, Midland & Scottish Railway served the territory described by its name. LMS Class 8F 2-8-0s were built beginning in 1935 for freight services. No. 48431 was photographed on the preserved Keighley & Worth Valley Railway. *Brian Solomon*

Opposite top: The 8F was among the best locomotives designed by the LMS's Sir William Stanier. It was mass-produced by no less than 11 different locomotive works in Britain. In addition to those locomotives serving the LMS and later British Railways, the type was exported to Italy and Middle Eastern countries. No. 48431 works upgrade toward the Mytholmes Tunnel near Haworth on the Keighley & Worth Valley Railway. *Brian Solomon*

Opposite bottom: The Worth Valley is best known as home to the famous Brontë sisters. Today, visitors also come to ride heritage trains, such as this one led by No. 48431. *Brian Solomon*

In 1936, the London & North Eastern Railway's highly praised chief mechanical officer, Sir Nigel Gresley (best known for his adaptation and perfection of the 4-6-2 Pacific type to British practice) applied his expert guidance in the development of a modern 2-6-2 type. The V2 prototype, class leader No. 4771, was built by the LNER's Doncaster Works in 1936. The type was deemed successful, and between 1936 and 1944, the LNER built a fleet of 184 V2s, dividing construction between its Doncaster and Darlington Works. *Brian Solomon*

Above: The LNER's pioneer V2, No. 4771, was named *Green Arrow* after the railway's fast freight service marketed under the same name. While such naming occasionally perplexes modern-day observers, at the time the naming logic was implicit, since the class V2 was designed to work fast freight. During World War II, the V2 class proved its value. The *Green Arrow* was preserved and still occasionally works main-line excursions. *Brian Solomon*

Left: The V2 was a three-cylinder simple locomotive. One key to its success was the casting of all three cylinders in a monoblock featuring carefully designed steam passages to ease flow of steam to the pistons. The central cylinder drove a crank axle. To reduce destructive dynamic forces, the V2 used lightweight alloyed-steel drive rods with precision counterbalanced drive wheels and reciprocating equipment. The last of the class was retired at the end of 1966. *Brian Solomon*

One of Britain's Big Four railways formed in 1923, the Southern Railway operated lines south and southwest of London. R. E. L. Maunsell, the Southern's first chief mechanical engineer, designed a number of 2-6-0s for passenger services, including the U class (Nos. 1610 to 1639). No. 1638 is a regular on the Bluebell Railway, one of the United Kingdom's pioneer preserved lines. Here, No. 1638 is seen ready to depart Sheffield Park with the Bluebell's high-end dining train, styled the *Golden Arrow* after the Southern's traditional continental express of the same name. *Brian Solomon*

Above: The Bluebell Railway was the first standard gauge preserved line in Britain and has rebuilt 9 miles of former Southern Railway secondary main line in East Sussex between Sheffield Park and Kingscote. Its premier excursion service is an all-Pullman dining train named after the Southern's *Golden Arrow*, seen here led by No. 1638 climbing the grade north of Horsted Keynes. The *Golden Arrow* re-creates a classic railway atmosphere for day-trippers visiting the line. *Brian Solomon*

Left: No. 1638 was built in 1931 and is one of two U-class 2-6-0s preserved on the Bluebell Railway. Bluebell, like most of Britain's finest preserved lines, protects train movements with a fully operational vintage signaling system. *Brian Solomon*

Above: Robert Fairlie's nineteenth-century twin-firebox articulated locomotive design was intended to provide the equivalent pulling power of a standard gauge locomotive. This narrow gauge locomotive was built in 1992 using the Fairlie patent and was named for David Lloyd George, Britain's prime minister from 1916 to 1922, who was of Welsh heritage. It works on the 13 1/2-mile Festiniog Railway in North Wales. *Brian Solomon*

Opposite top: The Festiniog Railway was a slate-hauling railway with exceptionally narrow tracks, just 1 foot 11 1/2 inches between rails. The line was preserved and today is one of several popular Welsh narrow gauge railways. *Brian Solomon*

Opposite bottom: No. 12 *David Lloyd George* leads a Festiniog train upgrade in the mountains of Wales near Dduallt. This distinctive articulated double-ended locomotive was common on some narrow gauge railways in Britain, Canada, Mexico, and South America. Pioneer American narrow gauge operator the Denver & Rio Grande even ordered one. *Brian Solomon*

Above: The Garratt type was built by Beyer Peacock in England and uses an unusual wheel arrangement whereby the whole weight of the locomotive is placed on the driving wheels while its boiler rides on a separate frame suspended between powered sections. This design allows for a relatively powerful locomotive with a big boiler that can operate through very tight curves. *Brian Solomon*

Right: The articulated Garratt was designed by Herbert W. Garratt and built in Manchester by Beyer Peacock for sale to railways around the world. Although never adopted in North America, the type was especially popular in Africa. Some have been used in Britain as well. *Brian Solomon*

North Wales is famous for its 2-foot-gauge railways. In addition to the pioneering Festiniog, numerous other small railways provide excursions using a variety of preserved locomotives. The Welsh Highland Railway at Caernarvon is a 2-foot-gauge line built on portions of an old standard gauge railway and on the alignment of the historic Welsh Highland. This articulated Garrett-type locomotive was built in England for service in South Africa. *Brian Solomon*

After a long day shoveling coal on the footplate, the Irish Rail's Ken Fox looks back over his train from the cab of No. 186 at Farranfore, County Kerry. The Great Southern & Western Railway's 101 class (also known as the J-15 class) 0-6-0 was a jack-of-all-trades and the most common locomotive on Irish railways until displaced by diesels in the 1950s and 1960s. *Brian Solomon*

Above: No. 186 is the oldest serviceable locomotive in Ireland. The design of the 101 class dates to 1867; No. 186 was built in November 1879. Here, it leads an excursion train at Farranfore, County Kerry, in 2006. The Railway Preservation Society of Ireland maintains several steam locomotives for excursion services in the Republic of Ireland and Northern Ireland. *Brian Solomon*

Left: Leading five Cravens-built passenger carriages and a generator van, No. 186 works east near Farranfore in May 2006. In the Victorian period, Ireland was under the yoke of Great Britain, and Irish railways were greatly influenced by their British counterparts. However, where British railways were largely built to Stephenson-standard 4-foot 8-1/2-inch gauge— also standard in the United States—Irish railways are broad gauge, built to 5 feet 3 inches. *Brian Solomon*

Although once the domain of several private companies, by the 1940s, Irish railways were insolvent and the government created a company called Córas Iompair Éireann (Irish Transport Company) to run rail, canal, and highway transport (buses) within the Republic of Ireland. No. 461 was built for the Dublin & South Eastern Railway and is seen here on the old Midland Great Western Railway line at Maynooth during a 1998 Railway Preservation Society of Ireland excursion. *Brian Solomon*

Irish railways remained relatively modest enterprises. Train size did not grow to even the proportions achieved by British counterparts. The largest locomotives were 4-6-0s, and most were substantially smaller. No. 461 was one of two inside-cylinder 2-6-0s built by Beyer Peacock in 1922 for goods (freight) services. It poses on the turntable at Mullingar, County Westmeath, with the Railway Preservation Society of Ireland crew and members of the Irish Rail staff. *Brian Solomon*

Safety valves lift on No. 461 as it waits "in the loop"—what would be called a passing siding in America— at Killucan for the passage of the evening train from Dublin's Connolly Station to Sligo. *Brian Solomon*

Above: Polish National Railways' (PKP) OL49 No. 169 is a heavy 2-6-2 designed for bidirectional running. Large coal reserves and intensive railway activity allowed main-line steam to survive longer in Poland than anywhere else in Europe. The last standard gauge steam roundhouse in regular use in Poland is at Wolsztyn, where privately sponsored locomotive driver (engineer) training has helped keep locomotives in action on regularly scheduled trains. *Brian Solomon*

Opposite top: On May 23, 2000, a PKP Class OL49 2-6-2 works a local freight at Grodzisk Wlkp, Poland. Regular steam-hauled freight services concluded in Poland in 2002, but select passenger trains from Wolsztyn have continued to use steam. *Brian Solomon*

Opposite bottom: Several Polish National Railways Class OL49 2-6-2s have been maintained in serviceable condition in recent years, both for regular passenger services from Wolsztyn and for excursions. In April 28, 2002, No. 111 leads a local train from Wolsztyn to Leszno, Poland. *Brian Solomon*

On a frosty morning at Jenbach, Austria, locomotive No. 4 is under steam and ready for its scheduled run over the narrow gauge Zillertalbahn-to-Mayrhofen. Zillertalbahn is a regional railway that provides regular passenger and freight services using modern diesel-powered equipment, though it operates seasonal steam trains as part of its regular timetable. *Brian Solomon*

Left: No. 4 works in an Alpine setting on its run up to Mayrhofen, Austria. Built by Krauss at Linz, Austria, in 1909, this locomotive worked for years on the Yugoslavian Railways (JZ) as No. JZ-83-076. It is considered a Class 83 and weighs 36 metric tons. *Brian Solomon*

Above: The Zillertalbahn crew prepares No. 4 at Jenbach on an abnormally cold January 2006 morning. This 0-8-2 type was typical of narrow gauge locomotives built for railways of the old Austrian-Hungarian Empire in the early years of the twentieth century. War and politics found the locomotive operating in the newly created Yugoslavia after 1918. *Brian Solomon*

Books

Beebe, Lucius, and Charles Clegg. *Narrow Gauge in the Rockies*. Berkeley, Calif.: Howell-North, 1958.

Best, Gerald M. *Snowplow: Clearing Mountain Rails*. Berkeley, Calif.: Howell-North, 1966.

Boyd, James I. C. *The Festiniog Railway, 1800–1974: Vol. 1, History and Route*. Usk, Mon, U.K.: The Oakwood Press, 1975.

———. *Festiniog Railway, 1800–1974. Vol. 2, Locomotives, Rolling*. Usk, Mon, U.K.: The Oakwood Press, 1975.

Bruce, Alfred W. *The Steam Locomotive in America: Its Development in the Twentieth Century*. New York: Norton, 1952.

Bush, Donald J. *The Streamlined Decade*. New York: Braziller, 1975.

Casserley, H. C. *Preserved Locomotives, 2nd Ed.* London: Ian Allan, 1968.

———. *The Observer's Directory of British Steam Locomotives*. London: Frederick Warne, 1980.

Clay, John F., and J. Cliffe. *The Stanier Black Fives*. London: Ian Allan, 1972.

———. *The West Coast Pacifics*. London: Ian Allan, 1976.

Conrad, J. David. *The Steam Locomotive Directory of North America: Vol. 1*. Polo, Ill.: Transportation Trails, 1988.

———. *The Steam Locomotive Directory of North America: Vol. 2*. Polo, Ill.: Transportation Trails, 1988.

Cook, Richard J. *Super Power Steam Locomotives*. San Marino, Calif.: Golden West, 1966.

Crump, Spencer. *Riding the Cumbres & Toltec Scenic Railroad*. Corona del Mar, Calif.: Zeta Publishers, 1992.

Dow, George. *British Steam Horses*. London: Phoenix House, 1950.

Drury, George H. *Guide to North American Steam Locomotives*. Waukesha, Wis.: Kalmbach Publishing 1993.

Dunscomb, Guy, L. *A Century of Southern Pacific Steam Locomotives, 1862–1962*. Modesto, Calif.: Dunscomb, 1963.

Ferrell, Mallory Hope. *Colorful East Broad Top*. Forest Park, Ill.: Heimburger House, 1995.

Forney, M. N. *Catechism of the Locomotive*. New York: Railroad Gazette, 1875.

Grenard, Ross, and Frederick A. Kramer. *East Broad Top to the Mines and Back*. Newton, N.J.: Carstens Publications, 1980.

Hauck, Cornelius W. *Colorado Rail Annual No. 10: Narrow Gauge to Central and Silver Plume: Route of the Famed Georgetown Loop*. Golden, Colo.: Colorado Rail Museum, 1972.

Hendry, R. Powell. *Narrow Gauge Story*. Rugby, U.K.: Hillside Publishing, 1979.

Hilton, George W. *American Narrow Gauge Railroads*. Palo Alto, Calif.: Stanford University Press, 1990.

LeMassena, Robert A. *Colorado's Mountain Railroads*. Golden, Colo.: Smoking Stack Press, 1963.

———. *Rio Grande . . . to the Pacific!* Denver: Sundance Publications, 1974.

McCoy, Dell A., and Russ Collman. *The Crystal River Pictorial*. Denver: Sundance Publications, 1972.

———. *The Rio Grande Pictorial, 1871–1971: One Hundred Years of Railroading thru the Rockies*. Denver: Sundance, 1971.

Mellander, Deane E. *East Broad Top: Slim Gauge Survivor*. Silver Spring, Md.: Old Line Graphics, 1995.

Morgan, David P. *Steam's Finest Hour*. Milwaukee, Wis.: Kalmbach Publishing, 1959.

———. *Locomotive 4501*. Milwaukee, Wis.: Kalmbach Publishing, 1968.

Nock, Oswald S. *The British Steam Railway Locomotive, 1925–1965*. Surrey, U.K.: Ian Allan, 1966.

———. *L.N.E.R. Steam*. London: A. M. Kelley, 1969.

———. *British Locomotives of the 20th Century, Vol. 2*. London: Stephens, 1984, 1985.

———. *British Locomotives of the 20th Century, Vol. 3: 1960 to the Present Day*. London: Guild, 1985.

Osterwald, Doris B. *Cinders & Smoke: A Mile by Mile Guide for the Durango to Silverton Narrow Gauge Trip*. Lakewood, Colo.: Western Guideways, 1982.

————. *Ticket to Toltec: A Mile by Mile Guide for the Cumbres & Toltec Scenic Railroad, 2nd Ed.* Denver, Western Guideways, 1992.

Quiett, Glenn Chesney. *They Built the West: An Epic of Rails and Cities.* New York: D. Appleton-Century, 1934.

Ransom, P. J. G. *Narrow Gauge Steam: Its Origins, Development and World-wide Influence.* Oxford: Oxford Publishing, 1996.

Ransome-Wallis, P. *World Railway Locomotives: The Concise Encyclopedia.* New York: Hutchinson, 1959.

Reid, Laurance S. *The Narrow Gauge Locomotives: The Baldwin Catalog of 1877.* Norman, Okla.: University of Oklahoma Press, 1967.

Ryan, Jeff, David McIntosh, and George Moon. *Working Steam: Stanier 8Fs.* London: Ian Allan, 2002.

Sinclair, Angus. *Development of the Locomotive Engine.* New York: D. Van Nostrand, 1907.

Smith, Warren L. *Berkshire Days on the Boston & Albany: The Steam Locomotives of the B&A, 1925–1950.* New York: Quadrant Press, 1982.

Solomon, Brian. *American Steam Locomotive.* Osceola, Wis.: Motorbooks International, 1998.

————. *The American Diesel Locomotive.* Osceola, Wis.: MBI Publishing, 2000.

————. *Super Steam Locomotives.* Osceola, Wis.: MBI Publishing, 2000.

————. *Locomotive.* St. Paul, Minn.: MBI Publishing, 2001.

Staufer, Alvin F. *C&O Power.* Carrollton, Ohio: Carrollton Printing, 1965.

Staufer, Alvin F., and Bert Pennypacker. *Pennsy Power II: Steam, Diesel and Electric Locomotives of the Pennsylvania Railroad.* Medina, Ohio: Wayner, 1968.

Staufer, Alvin F., and Edward L. May. *New York Central's Later Power, 1910–1968.* Medina, Ohio: Wayner 1981.

Swengel, Frank M. *The American Steam Locomotive: Vol. 1.* Davenport, Iowa: Midwest Rails Publications, 1967.

White, John H., Jr. *A History of the American Locomotive: Its Development, 1830–1880.* New York: Dover Publications, 1968.

————. *Early American Locomotives: With 147 Engravings.* New York: Dover Publications, 1972.

Wilson, O. Meredith. *The Denver and Rio Grande Project, 1870–1901: A History of the First Thirty Years of the Denver and Rio Grande Railroad.* Salt Lake City, Utah: Howe Brothers, 1982.

Wright, Richard K. *Southern Pacific Daylight, Vol. 1.* Thousand Oaks, Calif.: MHP Publications, 1970.

————. *America's Bicentennial Queen, Engine 4449: "The Lone Survivor".* Oakhurst, Calif.: Wright Enterprises, 1975.

Periodicals

Baldwin Locomotives. Philadelphia, Pa. [no longer published]

Classic Trains. Waukesha, Wis.

Jane's World Railways. London.

Journal of the Irish Railway Record Society. Dublin.

Locomotive & Railway Preservation. Waukesha, Wis. [no longer published]

RailNews. Waukesha, Wis. [no longer published]

Railroad History (formerly *Railway and Locomotive Historical Society Bulletin*). Boston.

Railway Age (variously *Railway Age Gazette*). Chicago and New York.

Railway Mechanical Engineer. New York. [no longer published]

Trains. Waukesha, Wis.

Vintage Rails. Waukesha, Wis. [no longer published]

5MT design, 167

A class, 15, 23, 68
Aberdine & Rockfish, 52
Alaculsy Lumber Company, 126
Allen, Horatio, 18
American Freedom Train, 115, 120
American Locomotive Company
(Alco), 14, 25, 34, 39, 52, 78,
84, 86, 111, 138, 142, 152
American type, 76, 149
Amtrak, 27
Atlantic type, 72, 73, 76
Austin Steam Train Association,
111

Baldwin Locomotive Works, 14, 39,
56, 57, 59, 62, 78, 90, 92, 97,
105, 121, 123, 128, 130–132,
134, 138, 140, 149, 150
Baltimore & Ohio (B&O), 16, 17,
33, 76, 114
Baltimore & Ohio Railroad
Museum, 15
Berkshire type, 35, 77, 98, 100, 101
Best Friend of Charleston, 18
Beyer Peacock, 178, 183
Big Boy type, 115, 150
Black Five, 166, 167
Blackmoor Vale, 164, 165
Blount, F. Nelson, 58
Blue Mountain & Reading, 28, 59
Bluebell Railway, 164, 165, 174,
175
Bocastle, 162, 163
Boone & Scenic Valley, 88, 89
Boston & Albany, 77, 101
Boston & Maine, 50
Braunschweig, Rick, 157
British Railways, 167, 170
Brooks Locomotive Works, 14, 111
Bulleid, O. V. S., 163
Burlington Northern, 76, 77, 108,
167

Burlington Northern Santa Fe, 108

California State Railroad Museum,
128, 148, 149, 151
Canadian Government Railways,
60
Canadian Locomotive Company,
45, 60
Canadian National Railway (CNR),
42, 44, 45, 50, 59, 60, 77
Canadian Pacific Railway (CPR),
58, 59, 61, 77
Central Pacific, 114
Central Railroad, 28, 29
Challenger type, 115, 154–156
Chesapeake & Ohio (C&O), 15,
30–36, 108
Chicago & North Western
(C&NW), 76, 94, 95, 152
Clay, Henry, 41
Claytor, W. Graham, 27
Climax Manufacturing Company,
15
Coal Processing Corporation, 126
Coast Line, 125
Colorado Railroad Museum, 134
Conrail, 43, 101
Consolidation type, 24, 29, 52, 76,
128
Conway Scenic Railway, 15, 50, 51
Cooper, Peter, 16, 17
Córas Iompair Eireann (Irish
Transport Company), 182
Cotton Belt, 106
Cravens, 181
CSX, 17
Cumbres & Toltec Scenic Railroad,
115, 136, 137, 144, 145, 147

Darlington Works, 172
David Lloyd George, 176
Davis, Phineas, 17
Daylight, 116, 117, 121
DDA40X, 157

Decapod type, 47, 114
Delaware & Hudson, 18, 58
Delaware, Lackawanna & Western,
95
Denver & Rio Grande Railway,
134, 135, 137, 176
Denver & Rio Grande Western
Railroad, 134, 138–140, 142
Dixiana, 127
Doncaster Works, 172
Dublin & South Eastern Railway,
182
Duluth & Northern Minnesota, 90
Duluth, Missabe & Iron Range,
104, 105
Durango & Silverton Narrow,
Gauge, 115, 138, 139, 142,
150

E2, 72
East Broad Top Railroad, 15,
62–67
Eggleston, Charles L., 117
Electro-Motive, 36
Employee Appreciation Special, 108
Erie Railroad, 30
Erlestoke Manor, 168, 169
Eureka, 150, 151
Eureka & Palisade, 150
Evening Star, 160

Fairlie, Robert, 176
Festiniog Railroad, 135, 161, 176,
179
Forney Transportation Museum, 95
Fox, Ken, 180
Friends of the 261, The, 78
Frisco, 108, 109

G-3-c, 58
Garratt, Herbert W., 178
Garratt type, 161, 178, 179
George, David Lloyd, 176
Gettysburg Railroad, 61

Golden Arrow, 174, 175
Grand Trunk Railway, 45, 50
Grange class, 168
Great Central Railway, 160, 162
Great Northern, 114
Great Southern & Western
    Railway, 161, 180
    101 class, 180, 181
Great Western Railway, 47, 160,
    168
Green Arrow, 173
Greenbrier, 31, 33
Gresley, Nigel, 163, 172
GS-4, 116, 117
Gulf Mobile & Northern, 59

H. K. Porter Company, 15, 39
Herber Creeper, 133
Hill Country Flyer, 111
Hudson, 77

Illinois Central, 77, 103
Irish Rail, 180

J class, 14, 20, 21, 23
J-15 class, 180
J-3a, 32, 35
Jablemann, Otto, 156
Jackson Iron and Steel Company,
    57
Juniata Shops, 73

K-27, 136, 137, 141, 146
K-28, 138, 141, 142
K-36, 115, 140–142, 144, 145
K-37, 141, 146
K4, 15, 70
Keighley & Worth Valley, 161, 170
Kentucky & Tennessee Railway, 26
Kettle Moraine Railway, 92, 93
King class, 168
Kingston Works, 60
Knoob, Earl, 133
Krauss, 187

Krieger, Bob, 155

L-1, 36, 70, 87, 106
Lake Superior & Ishpeming, 25, 90
Lake Superior Transportation
    Museum, 90
Lima Locomotive and Machine
    Company, 14
Lima Locomotive Works, 14, 34,
    77, 98, 100, 117, 126, 127
London & North Eastern Railway,
    160, 163, 172, 173
London, Midland & Scottish
    Railway, 160, 166, 167, 170
    Class 5, 166
    Class 8F, 170
Lowville & Beaver River Railroad,
    59

M class, 49
Maine Central, 50
Mallet type, 114
Manor class, 168
Maunsell, R. E. L., 174
McCloud River Railroad, 92, 130,
    131
Merchant Navy class, 163
Mid-Continent Railway Museum,
    95, 97
Middletown & Hummelstown
    (M&H), 42, 43
Midland Great Western Railway,
    182
Mikado, 15, 26, 52, 59, 60, 62, 64,
    66, 70, 76, 87, 88, 89, 90, 97,
    110, 111, 130, 131, 134, 136,
    138, 140, 146
Miller, E. L., 18
Millie, 64
Milwaukee Road, 76–78, 80, 81,
    86, 92
Minnesota Transportation
    Museum, 84
Mogul type, 42, 44, 76, 132, 133

Montreal Locomotive Works, 58
Morris, Joe Dale, 111
Mountain type, 108
Ms class, 27
Mudhen type, 136

National Railroad Museum, 80, 92
Nevada Central Railway, 149
New York Central, 76, 77, 98
New York, Susquehanna &
    Western, 15
Nickel Plate Road (NKP), 35, 76,
    77, 98–102
Niles Canyon Railway, 124
Norfolk & Western (N&W), 14,
    15, 20–23, 68, 69, 99
Norfolk Southern (NS), 15, 18,
    22, 99
North Pacific Coast, 149
North Shore Scenic Railroad, 90
North Star Rail Corporation, 78,
    80
Northern Pacific, 82–84, 105, 115
Northern type, 78, 115

O'Brien, Bernie, 58
Oregon Trail Special, 157
Overland type, 115

P-8, 121–123, 125
Pacific type, 58, 59, 70, 76, 121,
    125, 163, 172
Palmer, William Jackson, 135
Penn Central, 99
Pennsy Northern Central, 70
Pennsylvania Railroad (PRR), 14,
    15, 63, 70, 72, 76, 163
Pine Bluff Shops, 106
Pioneer Colliery, 41
Pioneer Tunnel Coal Mine, 41
Pocono type, 80
Polish National Railways (PKP),
    184
    Class OL49, 184

Polson Lumber Company, 97
Portland, Astoria & Pacific, 52
Prairie type, 52, 77, 93

R-1, 94, 95
Railfair Sacramento, 116, 122, 153
Railroad Museum of Pennsylvania,
    15, 44, 72, 73
Railway Preservation Society of
    Ireland, 161, 181–183
Reading & Northern, 15, 28
Reading Company, 15, 28, 29, 38,
    41, 42
Rio Grande Scenic Railroad, 115,
    133, 136, 141, 145–147
Roanoke Shops, 20, 69
Roaring Camp & Big Trees, 126,
    127
Rock Island, 76
Rocket, 17
Rogers Works, 84

S class, 35, 100
S-10, 84
S-2, 100
S-3, 78, 100
S-12, 131
Safe Harbor Water Power
    Corporation, 38, 39
Saginaw Timber Company, 96, 97
San Luis & Rio Grande, 133
Santa Fe Railway, 76, 77, 114
Santa Fe type, 114
Schenectady Locomotive Works, 14
Seaboard Coast Line, 27
Severn Valley Railway (SVR), 160,
    161, 166, 168, 169
Shay, Ephraim, 127
Shay type, 127
Sierra Railroad, 130, 131
Sierra Railway, 128, 129
Silverton Branch, 115
Sonoma, 148, 151
Soo Line, 83, 86, 87

South Carolina Railroad, 18
South Manchurian Railway, 84
Southern Pacific, 52, 106, 110, 111,
    114, 116–118, 120–123, 125,
    132, 153
Southern Railway, 15, 18, 26, 27,
    160, 162–164, 174, 175
Sport Models, 138
St. Charles Shops, 50
St. Louis & San Francisco, 108
St. Louis Southwestern, 106
Stanier, W. A., 166, 167, 170
Steamtown National Historic Site,
    15, 58–61, 80, 99
Stephenson, Robert, 17, 181
Strasburg Rail Road, 15, 42, 45–49,
    72, 73

T-1, 15, 28
Ten-Wheeler, 76, 83, 94, 95
Tennessee Valley Railroad
    Museum, 26
Texas type, 115
Toledo, Peoria & Western, 77, 103
Twelve-Wheeler, 114

U class, 174, 175
Union Pacific type, 115
Union Pacific, 77, 115, 150,
    152–157

V2 class, 172, 173
Valley Railroad, 15, 52
Virginia Museum of
    Transportation, 21, 22
Vulcan Iron Works, 15, 40

Wanamaker, Kempton & Southern,
    15, 38
Welsh Highland Railway, 161, 179
West Country Pacific type,
    162–165
West Country type, 163
West Point Foundry, 18

Western Maryland Scenic Railroad,
    15, 24, 25
Westinghouse, 82
White Pass & Yukon, 138
Whyte classification system, 11
0-6-0, 50, 51, 56, 57, 59, 115, 180
0-6-0T, 39
0-8-2, 187
2-4-0, 135
2-6-0, 42, 44, 76, 110, 132, 174,
    175, 183
2-6-2, 52, 77, 92, 93, 172, 184
2-6-6-2, 114
2-6-6-4, 68
2-10-2, 46, 114, 115
2-8-0, 24, 28, 52, 76, 110, 115, 128,
    129, 134, 146, 170
2-8-2, 52, 76, 87, 97, 110, 134
2-8-4, 77, 98, 100
2-8-8-4, 105
4-4-0, 42, 76, 149–151
4-4-2, 76
4-6-0, 76, 95, 110, 166–169, 183
4-6-2, 61, 76, 172
4-6-4, 36, 77
4-6-6-4, 115, 154
4-8-0, 49, 114
4-8-4, 15, 20, 28, 31, 35, 77, 78, 80,
    106, 108, 115, 118, 152, 153
4-8-8-4, 115
4-10-0, 114
4-10-2, 115
4-12-2, 115
Winans, Ross, 17
Wisconsin Central, 80
Woodard, Will, 98

Yellowstone type, 105
Yreka Western, 130
Yugoslavian Railways (JZ), 187
    Class 83, 187

Zephyr, 167
Zillertalbahn, 161, 186, 187